MW01274154

Case Studies in International Management

Case Studies in International Management

Christopher Sawyer-Lauçanno

Massachusetts Institute of Technology

REGENTS/PRENTICE HALL, Englewood Cliffs, New Jersey 07632

Library of Congress Cataloging-in-Publication Data

Sawyer-Lauçanno, Christopher
 Case studies in international management.

 1. International business enterprises—
Management—Case studies. I. Title.
HD62.4.S29 1987   658'.049   86–22724
ISBN 0-13-119298-1

Cover design: Ben Santora
Manufacturing buyer: Carol Bystrom

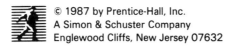 © 1987 by Prentice-Hall, Inc.
A Simon & Schuster Company
Englewood Cliffs, New Jersey 07632

Printed in the United States of America

10 9 8 7

ISBN 0-13-119298-1

Prentice-Hall International (UK) Limited, *London*
Prentice-Hall of Australia Pty. Limited, *Sydney*
Prentice-Hall Canada Inc., *Toronto*
Prentice-Hall Hispanoamericana, S.A., *Mexico*
Prentice-Hall of India Private Limited, *New Delhi*
Prentice-Hall of Japan, Inc., *Tokyo*
Prentice-Hall of Southeast Asia Pte. Ltd., *Singapore*
Editora Prentice-Hall do Brasil, Ltda., *Rio de Janeiro*

Contents

Preface

This book contains ten case studies dealing with various situations in international management. Although all of the cases are based on actual incidents that real companies have encountered, they have all been altered somewhat to protect the confidentiality of the information. The names of all the companies and individuals, for example, are fictitious; in addition, the exhibits have been rewritten and edited, and in some cases, condensed, expanded, or created, and in two of the case studies the specific products have been changed to prevent identification. Despite these alterations, the issues are genuine and have been chosen because they illustrate important aspects of international business.

Two common themes tie these case studies together: their international nature and the prominence of English as a language of worldwide communication. The aim of the text is to enable intermediate and advanced students of English to learn about the world of business while they improve their fluency in speaking, reading, writing, and listening.

The case study method, widely used at American business schools and in corporate training, has been chosen because it does more than just provide business information. It involves the participants in actual problem solving, a process that is a major part of managerial practice. The key in dealing with these cases, therefore, is involvement. Not enough can be said for active participation. It is absolutely the most important element both in improving English and in mastering the material in the case. If a case is studied and discussed fully and earnestly, the results can be quite rewarding. Not only will case study lead to sharper English language skills, it will also provide real knowledge of international business problems and practices.

Acknowledgments

The author wishes to thank the following individuals who greatly helped in the preparation of this text: A. Akoto, S. Brooke, C. Y. Chen, M. El-Kadi, R. Garcia, E. Grindel, K. Hozaki, S. Kurokawa, A. Larbi, J. Rosa, D. Wilson, and W. Woo. I am especially grateful to my graduate students at the Massachusetts Institute of Technology; their own exceptional efforts and insights about these cases taught me, even as I taught them.

To the Instructor

Although detailed lesson-by-lesson guidance is provided in the Instructor's Manual, a few words are useful to describe the overall intent of the book. This text is designed for high-intermediate to advanced learners of English as a second/foreign language. The focus of the text, international business, presupposes an interest in learning "business English" but does not require extensive knowledge of business practices on the part of either the student or the instructor. This does not mean that the issues in the case are necessarily simple, only that the actual business content of the cases is generally not so sophisticated as to be overpowering. Specific business notes, however, are contained in the Instructor's Manual in order to facilitate your teaching of the case.

The case study method itself, although associated primarily with U.S. business schools, is gradually becoming more prominent in advanced ESL/EFL classes. The reasons for the adoption of the method are numerous. First, it fosters active communication. Because a case study is essentially an exercise in problem solving, students must work together to arrive at a solution or solutions to the dilemma. Participation, therefore, becomes natural. Second, since students are continually "put on the spot" to present ideas and defend positions in English, the case method promotes thinking in the language. Third, because case studies do not overtly scream "English," the resistance of some students is greatly reduced. Finally, the case study method reorients the classroom so that the primary responsibility is placed on the students, rather than on the teacher. This most often results in a dynamic learning situation in which motivation comes from within rather than from without.

These attributes of the case method do not come automatically. Thorough preparation by both the instructor and students is important for success. Before launching the discussion/simulation, an instructor should review the basic facts of the case with the students, clarifying vocabulary and examining aspects of grammar and usage. The discussion questions that follow each case are designed to aid the student in uncovering the main facts, as well as the connections between the various case parts. The questions may be assigned as written homework or may simply serve as the basis for the initial review by the instructor.

While the case is being discussed, the instructor must be willing to cede the authoritative role and become an informed guide, making sure that the students do not stray from the relevant facts in the case. Error correction should be kept to a minimum in order to avoid impeding the communication. This does not mean, however, that mistakes should be ignored. A few minutes at the end of class can be used to point out errors made during the activity.

Error correction can also be handled quite effectively through the post–case study application exercises. These follow-up exercises (such as writing letters, memos, or case summaries; expanding notes; interpreting graphs or charts; inventing dialogues and role plays) help to cement the learning while contributing to the student's study of the case.

Although it is difficult to determine how much class time should be allocated per case study, I have found, as have others who have class-tested the cases, that a minimum of three hours is generally needed. In classes in which students are less well prepared, class time could be profitably extended to four or even six hours. It should be noted here that lower-level classes, while needing more linguistic guidance from the instructor, are still able to gain a great deal from the cases.

Some of the cases in this book are somewhat controversial; some are fairly technical; all of them, I hope, are interesting. They are arranged in order of difficulty—"difficulty" as defined from a business point of view. The linguistic level is fairly constant, although the last five cases introduce more complex sentence structures and rely, to some extent, on the vocabulary acquired in the first five cases. The instructor should feel free, however, to pick and choose the cases according to interest, business situation, or practical application.

For the instructor who wants to select cases by subject, here is a breakdown of the case studies by content area:

International Sales/Marketing: Case 4, Leclerc Machines de Cuisine; Case 6, Harding Tool Corporation; Case 7, Comtec Corporation; Case 9, International Carpet Wholesalers; Case 10, Yoon-Choi Corporation.

Management/Personnel/Cultural Conflicts: Case 1, Fitzburg Tire Company; Case 2, Wilson Chemicals (Ghana) Ltd.; Case 3, Millars Bank Ltd.; Case 8, Hanover Public Systems; Case 9, International Carpet Wholesalers.

International Trade/Joint Ventures: Case 2, Wilson Chemicals (Ghana) Ltd.; Case 4, Leclerc Machines de Cuisine; Case 5, Tanaka Komuten Company, Ltd.; Case 6, Harding Tool Corporation; Case 8, Hanover Public Systems; Case 9, International Carpet Wholesalers.

The cases can also be broken down by geographic areas. It should be noted, however, that while some of the cases contain geographically specific information, the problems themselves can be applied to a wide variety of situations in practically an unlimited number of geographic settings.

Experience has shown that these case studies can be profitably used for a wide range of business English training courses. As a self-contained text, the book is highly useful for introducing students to the actual language and practice of business while at the same time giving them an opportunity to practice their skills. As part of a larger set of business materials, it can both complement and expand considerably the existing curriculum.

How to Study a Case

The case studies in this text all have three main parts: background, dialogue, and exhibits and supporting materials. To develop a thorough knowledge of a case, you will need first to examine each section carefully. Next, you should put the facts from one section together with the facts from the other sections in order to form a comprehensive understanding of the case problem.

To help you in doing this, let's look at each of the main parts. The background, as the name implies, contains general background information about the situation, the company, and the people involved. Some students have found it useful to make a list of the main facts they can learn from the background. The headings and subheadings of a typical list might look something like this:

I. What I know about the company
   A. Type of company
   B. Products
   C. Location
   D. Size
   (If the case involves more than one company, you could repeat this information for the second company.)
II. What I know about the people in the case
   A. Name
   B. Position
   C. Other information (how long with the company, attitudes, accomplishments)
   (Repeat for each key figure.)

III. What I know about the problem in the case
- A. Chronology of events
  1. This happened first
  2. This happened next
  3. Then this happened
  4. This finally happened
- B. Main issues
  1. Quantitative aspects (financial, marketing, sales, production data)
  2. Qualitative aspects (attitudes, emotions, conflicts)

Since each case is unique, the details in your lists will undoubtedly vary from case to case. This basic format, however, should help you organize the essential information you have learned from the background. When making your list, be sure to leave plenty of extra space so that information from the other sections can be added.

The dialogue in the cases serves three main purposes: (1) it adds factual information to the case, (2) it gives you important knowledge of the emotions and attitudes of the people involved, and (3) it provides you with an opportunity to see how English is actually and naturally spoken.

The dialogue often supplies you with significant facts that cannot be learned from any of the other materials in the case. When reading the dialogue, take careful note of how the individuals relate to one another. Is their relationship formal or informal? What aspect of the case is most important to them? Try to categorize their basic positions regarding the situation.

Also check the dialogue for subtle statements or shifts in the conversation. These can often reveal important clues that might be useful to you in analyzing the case problem. In Case 1, for example, the dialogue tells us a great deal about the personalities and, in turn, the central problem in the case. The American manager, Bierman, is upset and wants to point blame. His Mexican associate, Sánchez García, is calm but defensive. Bierman's questions are antagonistic: "So whose fault was it?" "Can he read?" Sánchez García, on the other hand, attempts to reassure Bierman that while the project is not on schedule, it is going to be all right in the end. From this conversation it is fairly clear what the major problem in the case really is: a conflict of cultures, values, and personalities.

Once you have finished reading the dialogue you should have a good sense of how the individuals in the case feel about the problem with which they are involved. At this point, go back and make some additions to your original fact list.

You will now want to look at the exhibits and supporting materials section. The documents in this section contribute further to the case. When studying the exhibits, bear in mind that they present you with information in an indirect fashion. It is up to you to decide how the exhibit fits into the case and how it expands your knowledge.

Some of the documents will be far more useful than others; don't feel that each exhibit must be equally informative. Regardless of the content and value to the case, however, each exhibit provides an example of an actual business document and can serve as a model of English business communication. As you study each exhibit, remember to add the new information to your fact list.

Once you have finished studying the exhibits and supporting materials and have read over the information in the section titled Some Points to Keep in Mind, you will be ready to come to a conclusion about the case itself. Using the information jotted down on your fact list—combined with the opinions, ideas, and facts gained from in-class discussions—you should now be able to use profitably the section called Checklist and Worksheet. The checklist should be used to help you remember important facts and make sure you have taken the major factors in the case into consideration.

All that you now have to do is make a final decision about what should be done to solve the problem(s) in the case. For this you will want to review all the facts. Make your decision on the basis of all that you know about the situation. It is not important that everyone have the same answer. In fact, there is no *one* correct answer. If you have based your decision on what you know about the case and have used those facts to guide you to a reasonable solution, you will always be right.

When studying a case you may find that some of the information is difficult to understand. If this happens, don't get discouraged. Make some notes about what you find confusing and bring your questions to class. At the same time, try to interpret the case as well as you can. What isn't understandable on a first reading will often become clearer after further study.

Above all, be willing to share your ideas and to listen to the insights and comments of others. Studying cases can be an enjoyable, stimulating, and highly practical way to improve your English while also learning about the world of international management.

Case Studies in International Management

Fitzburg Tire Company

BACKGROUND

It was a beautiful Sunday afternoon in the spring of 1984. For Max Bierman, the American construction manager of his company's partially completed Fitzburg Tire Company plant in Cuernavaca, Mexico, though, it was a bad day. He had spent the afternoon reviewing the project and was clearly upset. Construction was already three months behind schedule, costs were in excess of those projected, and his chief engineer, Leopoldo Sánchez García, had reported on Friday that most of the work completed in the last three weeks had to be redone because it failed to meet specification. It seemed to Bierman that never before had he had so many problems at one time.

This was not the first plant that Bierman had built for Fitzburg, but it was the first one he had supervised outside the U.S. At first Bierman had been delighted with Mexico. Cuernavaca was a beautiful city in the mountains, the people seemed friendly, and his accommodations—a huge house with servants and swimming pool—were superior to his home in the United States.

The problems with the plant, however, had begun to change his attitudes. In uncharacteristic fashion, he began to blame Mexican workers, Mexican supervisors, Mexican bureaucracy, in short, everything Mexican, for the difficulties. Even his "right-hand man," Sánchez García, seemed to have failed him. To compound matters, Bierman's monthly progress report was due in a few days at the head office in Philadelphia. It appeared that once again he would have to file a "nonprogress" report, which justifiably would concern his superiors. After one hour of deliberating what to do, he picked up the telephone and called Sánchez García at home.

DIALOGUE: A PLANNING SESSION

CAST: Max Bierman, Construction Manager, Fitzburg Tire Co., Cuernavaca

Leopoldo Sánchez García, Chief Engineer, Fitzburg Tire Co., Cuernavaca

Ing.* Sánchez García and Mr. Bierman are meeting in a restaurant late Sunday afternoon to discuss and develop solutions for the problems at Fitzburg Tire Company.

Bierman: Sorry to drag you out on a Sunday afternoon, Leopoldo, but we've got some problems that have to get settled, and settled quickly.

Sánchez: You're referring to the mixing pit walls that have to be taken down and done again.

Bierman: Well, we might as well start with that.

Sánchez: Okay. As I told you on Friday, the problem is with the H-steel reinforcements. There should be twice as many pylons for the pit to be structurally sound.

Bierman: So whose fault was it?

Sánchez: It's not a question of fault or blame. I suppose I'm to be blamed for going on vacation. The *maestro,* Muñoz, is to be blamed for not following directions; John is to be blamed for not keeping a close eye on the operation. But in the end, it doesn't matter, it has to be redone.

Bierman: What's wrong with Muñoz anyway? This isn't the first time he's made a mistake.

Sánchez: Max, what you need to understand is that these workers need a lot of supervision. You can't manage this kind of construction from the office.

Bierman: Can he read?

Sánchez: Who?

Bierman: Muñoz. John told me he can't read.

Sánchez: He can read, and he's not stupid. But he is a subcontractor,

---

*Ing. is an abbreviation for *Inginiero* (engineer). In Latin America professionals often use their title in place of Mr., Miss, or Mrs.

and he thought he could cut a corner and save some expense by only using half the amount of steel.

Bierman: So let's get rid of him. There are a lot of people out there who can do the job.

Sánchez: It's not that simple. Muñoz is good. I told him on Friday he'll have to rip up the concrete and do the job right.

Bierman: But the delays! We're already so far behind schedule.

Sánchez: I know, but it's better to do it right.

Bierman: I'm not saying not to do it right. What I'm saying is that the situation is out of control. John agrees.

Sánchez: Neither John nor you have experience in Mexico. I told you at the beginning that your time schedule was unrealistic. Things are not as bad as they seem.

Bierman: Oh yeah? What am I going to tell Philadelphia on Wednesday—that this is the land of *mañana,* where time schedules don't matter?

Sánchez: Yes, to some extent you'll have to tell them that. But you'll also have to show them that when this plant is done, it will be a model for Fitzburg plants everywhere. Max, it is being built right.

Bierman: How can you say that? Leopoldo, I'm going to have to make some changes. Up to now I've listened to you, trusted your judgment, believed that you knew how to handle your people. But it's not working. And besides, we're not running a charity organization. We've got jobs that people need, and I want you to make sure that the people who have jobs deserve them. I also want you to tighten up operations. This whole siesta business is ridiculous. Orders aren't delivered on time, crews don't show up. Leopoldo, you've got to get this under control.

Sánchez: Max, I understand your frustration and agree things can be improved. But at the same time having a hostile attitude toward the workers isn't going to do anything for anyone.

Bierman: I'm not hostile toward the workers. I just want to see some visible progress made without hitches, without delays, without cost overruns. I want you to make the changes as you see fit, but I want changes. I want people working, not standing around leaning on the machinery. I want things done right the first time, not the second or third time. I want to increase the work tempo, I want changes, and I want results.

Sánchez: I'll see what I can do, but, Max, you have to remember that in Mexico things are done differently. I've been building plants in this country and in Latin America for thirty years. You've been here less than a year.

Bierman: I know. I trust you. I recognize that there will be differences. But you see the spot I'm in, don't you? Philadelphia could care less about our problems. They just want a plant built and running within a reasonable time period. And that's our job. Nothing less, nothing more.

EXHIBITS AND SUPPORTING MATERIALS

Exhibit I. Memo from Sánchez García to Max Bierman

```
                    Interoffice Memorandum

   TO: Max Bierman
   FM: Leopoldo Sánchez García
   DT: April 29, 1984
   RE: Procedural changes


   In response to our conversation of yesterday afternoon, I have
   initiated the following changes:

   1. I warned Maestro Miguel Muñoz that another mistake would result in
      his immediate termination for breach of contract. (I doubt if this
      is legal, but I think it sufficiently provoked a more responsive
      attitude.) Demolition of the retaining wall was begun at the
      expense of Maestro Muñoz. A new wall should be in place by May 3rd.

   2. I spoke with Juan Carillo in personnel about hiring thirty more
      unskilled workers. They would be used to supplement the existing
      work crews. He said he could probably have them on the job within a
      week. This would greatly speed up initial construction.

   3. Abolishing the 90-minute siesta break is impossible. It simply
      flies in the face of tradition. Since the workers put in eight-hour
      days anyway, I don't see that it matters much whether they work from
      8:00-4:30 or from 8:00-6:00.

   4. An obvious problem exists with the use of too many subcontractors.
      Because of legal entanglements, we are stuck with them at present. A
      logical solution, though, is to hire three or four young engineers
      to supervise them closely. This would alleviate the problem to a
      very great extent.
```

Exhibit 2. Memo from Max Bierman to Sánchez García

From the Desk of Max Bierman

Leopoldo, you haven't gotten the message. Your so-called ''changes''
amount to nothing at all. The answer is not to hire more workers, either
unskilled or engineers. The answer is to get people who are on the job
working! And about the siesta break—the workers begin to slow down an
hour before siesta and take at least an hour to get back in full swing.
We're losing two hours a day of full-work productivity. Whether
traditional or not, it's got to go. Work tempo has to be increased, and
costs have to remain the same.

Exhibit 3. Bierman's Progress Report to the Head Office

Fitzburg Tire Co., S.A. de C.V.
Apartado Postal 96
Cuernavaca, Morelos, Mexico

May 1, 1984

TO: Ann Block, V.P., Overseas Operations
FROM: Max Bierman, General Construction Manager, Cuernavaca
SUBJECT: April Progress Report

This report covers the period from April 1 to April 30, 1984, regarding
the construction of the Fitzburg Tire Plant in Cuernavaca, Mexico.

Summary of Work Previously Completed

From the beginning of construction in August 1983, the foundations for
the main assembly facility, curing room, and storage rooms have been
laid and the basic frame for all facilities erected.

Work Completed—April 1–April 30

Major tasks during this time period have been confined to continued work on the erection of the structural frames, on reinforcement (with H–shape steel covered with concrete) of the internal mixing pits, and on preparation for installation of the tire–building machines and milling machines. Some delays were experienced because of procurement problems (the steel arrived one week late), which were compounded by construction errors on the part of the subcontractor building the mixing pits. The latter problem has been corrected, and the pits are nearing completion.

Work Scheduled—May 1–May 31

Continued work on the external frames, completion of the mixing pits, reinforcement of the platforms for machinery installation (extruders, tire–building drums, molds), and completion of the storage rooms.

Budget

See appendix.

Proposed Changes

In order to combat cost overruns and the slow construction progress, a number of changes will be instituted this month:

1.   Tighter fiscal and supervisory control will be placed over the subcontractors. Accountability for meeting deadlines and for the quality of workmanship will be increased.

2.   Work tempo will be increased by abolishing siesta break (a 90–minute interlude in the middle of the day). In its place, all workers, including subcontractors and their crews, will be placed on an eight–hour day with a thirty–minute lunch break.

3.   John Perkins, my assistant, will be put in charge of ensuring that these changes are efficiently implemented. He will work with the project's chief engineer/construction supervisor, Leopoldo Sánchez García.

It is firmly believed that these changes will help put the Cuernavaca construction project back on line, both in terms of costs and schedule. The outlook for the future is considerably brighter.

cc: J. Perkins
      L. Sánchez García

Exhibit 4. Memo from Sánchez García to Max Bierman

```
                         MEMORANDUM


    TO:      Max
    FROM:    Leopoldo
    SUBJECT: Progress Report
    DATE:    May 2, 1984


    Max,

    Your proposed changes won't work. You won't gain a thing from doing
    away with the siesta. In fact, all you'll gain from this is a lot of ill
    will. Cooperation with the workers is needed, not hostility.

    John, while a good engineer, is not the person to be in charge of
    overseeing efficiency. His inability to communicate in Spanish is a
    major handicap and can result only in mutual misunderstanding. As it
    is, he is not particularly liked by the workers, being perceived as a
    young, inexperienced "Americano" with no sense of actual
    construction. If he is put in the role of watchdog, we'll be in real
    trouble.

    Max, this is Mexico, not the United States. You can't run a project the
    same way here as you can in the U.S. Just the differences in equipment,
    materials, and methods are alone sufficient reason to adopt different
    tactics. I'll do what I can to improve efficiency and reduce costs, but
    you can't impose efficiency on anyone. The workers and subcontractors
    have to be educated in new methods of building, not given ultimatums.

    Please reconsider your changes. Let me handle it, my way. Let's talk
    when you get back from Mexico City.



                         Leopoldo
```

Handwritten annotations:

strategy 战略，策略

siesta [siéstə] 午睡
hostility [hɔstíliti] 敌对行为
oversee 监督 v.
overseer 工头 n.
handicap [hǽndikæp] 障碍
mutual [mjúːtjuəl] 相互的
tactics [tǽktik] 策略 (技巧方法)
impose [impóuz] 强加 v.
ultimatum [ʌltiméitəm] 最后通牒 n.

Some Points to Keep in Mind

Inefficiency, delays, cost overruns—these are the problems Bierman names as being responsible for his "proposed changes." He is justifiably upset, and yet as Sánchez García notes, "You can't impose efficiency on anyone." The central issue in this case, then, is whether Bierman can expect Mexican workers (and supervisors) to "play by the rules of his game."

There is ample evidence to support an argument that this case has nothing to do with American versus Mexican ways. The project is behind schedule, costs are high, and inefficiency is present. Certainly, these problems are not unique to Mexico. Bierman's response, however, is to see the issue as a clash of cultures, to blame the siesta for his troubles, to blame the Mexican employees for not working hard enough. His solution, as a result, is to try to impose an American-style workday on the project, forcing the workers to conform to his way of doing things. Sánchez García, on the other hand, sees the situation as one in which more workers and understanding are needed to get the job done correctly.

Is either right? Is the solution as simple as either man sees it? What will be the consequences of Bierman's changes? Are these changes really addressing the problem, or are they external to it?

解决   米在68

CHECKLIST AND WORKSHEET

In coming to a decision about this case, did you consider the following?

> The obvious inefficiency
>
> Bierman's attitude
>
> Bierman's proposed changes
>
> Sánchez García's ideas (Exhibits 1 and 4)
>
> The consequences of Bierman's proposed actions

What other factors should be considered?

_____

_____

_____

_____

Decision:

_____

_____

_____

_____

DISCUSSION QUESTIONS

The purpose of these questions is to promote better understanding of the basic facts, issues, and language of the case. They should be answered, in either written or oral form, after the entire case has been read, but before the class discussion.

I. Background and Dialogue
   1. Describe Bierman. What are his attitudes toward the project, Mexico, and Mexicans? How have these attitudes changed since he arrived in Cuernavaca? Support your description with specific references to the case.
   2. Describe Sánchez García. How would you characterize his relationship with Bierman? With the workers?
   3. What is the specific problem that has caused Bierman to meet with Sánchez García on Sunday? How does that problem relate to the general problem in the case?
   4. What is a siesta? Why does Bierman want to change the practice? Why does Sánchez García defend it?

II. Exhibits and Supporting Materials
   1. Is the memo in Exhibit 1 truly a response to the conversation on Sunday? If so, how? If not, why not?
   2. Contrast Exhibit 1 with Exhibit 2. Which memo is in formal style? What is the difference in tone between them? Which memo seems more professional? Why? Support your answers with specific references to the memos.
   3. Analyze Exhibit 3. How does Bierman attempt to explain the delays? What is the purpose of the last section, Proposed Changes?
   4. Why does Sánchez García write the memo in Exhibit 4? Given the tone of this memo, do you think that Bierman consulted Sánchez García about the progress report?

EXERCISES

I. In reading this case, you probably encountered a number of words that were unfamiliar to you. Sometimes the easiest and quickest way to find out what a word means is to look it up in the dictionary. Often, however, a word may actually be defined through the context in which it is used. Whenever possible, use the latter method to discover what a word means.

Look at the following example taken from the Background:

> . . . the people seemed friendly, and his *accommodations*—a huge house with servants and swimming pool—were superior to his home in the United States.

You may not have known the word *accommodations*. Notice, however, that a description of what the accommodations were immediately follows the use of the word. From the description, it is fairly obvious that the *accommodations* are the house and services furnished Bierman.

In the following exercises, read over the sentences taken from the case. Then, using the contextual clues, choose the *best* definition.

1. It's not a question of *fault* or blame.
    a. accident
    b. wrongdoing
    c. favor
2. He thought he could *cut a corner* and save some expense by only using half the amount of steel.
    a. economize
    b. do something right
    c. criticize
3. Some delays were experienced because of *procurement* problems (the steel arrived one week late).
    a. personnel
    b. construction
    c. acquisition
4. Work *tempo* will be increased by abolishing siesta break.
    a. temporary
    b. pace
    c. methods
5. In fact, all you'll gain from this is a lot of *ill will*. Cooperation with the workers is needed, not hostility.
    a. resentment
    b. understanding
    c. willfulness
6. His inability to communicate in Spanish is a major *handicap* and can result only in mutual misunderstanding.
    a. advantage

b. interest

c. disadvantage

7. Abolishing the 90-minute siesta break is impossible. It simply *flies in the face of* tradition.

   a. disregards

   b. is a factor in

   c. is similar to

8. A logical solution, though, is to hire three or four young engineers. This would *alleviate* the problem to a very great extent.

   a. worsen

   b. excuse

   c. lessen

9. So let's *get rid of* him. There are a lot of people out there who can do the job.

   a. promote

   b. reward

   c. fire

10. These workers need a lot of *supervision*. You can't manage this kind of construction from the office.

    a. overseeing

    b. care

    c. incentives

II. Expand the following notes about Bierman into complete sentences. You might have to refer to the Background section for some of the information.

Example: Bierman/construction manager/Cuernavaca/plant

Max Bierman was the construction manager at the Cuernavaca plant.

1. Bierman/worried/project

2. first/Bierman/delighted

3. report/few days/Philadelphia

4. problems/change/attitude

_____

5. seemed/never/problems

_____

6. Bierman/decided/Sánchez García

_____

III. Expand the dialogue between Bierman and Sánchez García. Use the information from the case to help you.

Bierman: Sorry to drag you out on a Sunday afternoon, Leopoldo.

Sánchez: _____

_____

Bierman: We've got some problems that have to get settled.

Sánchez: _____

_____

Bierman: Basically, that things don't get done right, or on time.

Sánchez: _____

_____

Bierman: Well, in the majority of cases, it is.

Sánchez: _____

_____

Bierman: Yes, that's right. Muñoz is a good example of what I'm talking about.

Sánchez: _____

_____

IV. Look at the following project chart and write a brief paragraph contrasting the actual progress with the projected progress. You can use some of the terms from the progress report (Exhibit 3) to help you with the vocabulary.

1983

	Apr.	May	June	July	Aug.	Sept.	Oct.	Nov.	Dec.
Projected	site selection	earth-moving	lay foundation		erect framework		install wiring & piping	pour concrete floor slabs	
Actual	site selection	earth-moving	foundation laid				framework erected		

V. Prepare a response in the form of a memo from Bierman to Sánchez García regarding Exhibit 4. Use the memos in the case as examples of format and style.

VI. Perform the following guided role plays. In role plays, one student takes the role of one of the characters, another student the role of another character, etc. The students then rehearse, with careful attention being paid to what is actually known about the situation and about the character. During the rehearsals, the students should attempt to develop the basic focus of the role play, but should not write out the dialogue lines. Once the students have formulated their positions, the role plays can be performed for the class. The instructor should limit the amount of time spent by the students both in rehearsing and performing the role plays.
  1. Bierman and Sánchez García are meeting for lunch to discuss the Fitzburg construction at these times:
  a. before the April progress report
  b. after the April progress report
  c. after Bierman's "proposed changes" have gone into effect
  2. Bierman and Sánchez García are meeting with Ann Block, Vice-President for Overseas Operations. They are explaining the project and the reason for the delays.

    3. John Perkins, Bierman's assistant, is meeting with Sánchez García to ask his advice about how to proceed with getting the project back on schedule.

VII. The class is divided into two groups for debates. One group is assigned a "for" position, the other group an "against" position. The groups should be given some time to prepare their positions. If the instructor elects to make the debate a formal one, then members of the groups may be assigned responsibility for debate sequences such as opening statement, first rebuttal, second rebuttal, and closing statement. Even if the debate is not to be conducted in a formal manner, each student should be responsible both for formulating and delivering part of the argument. It is important that each student get an opportunity to participate in the activity. Debate one of the following questions:

    1. Is Sánchez García covering up real supervision problems with the phrase, "You just don't understand Mexico."?

    2. Should Bierman fire Sánchez García?

    3. Is Bierman too intolerant of the host culture?

VIII. Write an analysis of the situation from the viewpoint of either Sánchez García, Bierman, or the Philadelphia head office. Make sure you back up your analysis with facts from the case.

2 Wilson Chemicals (Ghana) Ltd.

BACKGROUND

Wilson Chemicals (Ghana) Ltd., a subsidiary of the British company Wilson Chemicals, was a Ghanian manufacturer of chemicals, particularly chemical fertilizers. Since its establishment in 1952 the subsidiary had grown at a steady rate despite the economic difficulties and political upheavals since independence. There were several reasons for its success. First, its primary product was fertilizers, which were in great demand in this agriculturally based economy. Second, it had since 1958 been responsive to the host country by employing more and more native Ghanians in top positions. Third, in 1972 it had named Mr. Joseph Okono, an Oxford-educated Ghanian, as subsidiary president, thus removing the last vestige of "colonial" control.

Mr. Okono proved to be an extremely able manager: he had increased sales on an average of 10 percent a year, tripled real profits, seemed to have a flair for working cooperatively with whatever government was in power, and was well liked by employees and clients alike.

In the winter of 1984, however, a careful examination by a British-based auditing firm revealed enormous discrepancies in accounting practices. In short, it appeared that Mr. Okono, during the last year, had used about £50,000 as "incentives" to bureaucrats in government agencies (the chief purchasers of fertilizers) to gain key contracts, minimize bureaucratic red tape, and generally streamline procedures. In London the directors of the corporation were naturally worried about the news but were unsure of what course of action to pursue.

15

DIALOGUE: A POLICY DISCUSSION

CAST: George Teele, Vice President, International Division, Wilson Chemicals

Gerald Howard, President, Wilson Chemicals

Ian Thomas, Director, West African Division, Wilson Chemicals

The directors are meeting at the London head office to discuss the news received from the independent auditors in Accra, Ghana.

Thomas: Gentlemen, I'll come right to the point. Mr. Okono must be fired. We cannot allow this situation to endure any longer than it has.

Howard: How long has it been going on?

Thomas: Who knows? Certainly for some time, I should think.

Teele: All we know is that about £50,000 were used for "incentives" in 1983.

Thomas: Incentives, bribes, call them what you like, but what we have here is a clear case of dishonesty.

Howard: I'm not so sure there is any "clear case" at all. We all know that business is done differently from place to place, and I really have no reason to assume that Mr. Okono is not simply conducting business the way it must be conducted to ensure growth.

Teele: That's right. And what we also have to look at here is not what Mr. Okono has done wrong, but what he's done right. Profits are way up, and problems are down. Given the continual economic and social/political disorders, I'd say that Mr. Okono has done a fine job. It's not that I'm justifying bribery, but let's be honest—we all know it exists, and until the audit none of us could really care less how Mr. Okono managed to triple profits.

Howard: Well, I don't know if I'd go so far to say "we couldn't care less," but it is true we were more interested in the end than in the means.

Thomas: Let us assume that as far as we are concerned Mr. Okono has a free hand to distribute gratuities to whomever he desires. But there is another problem.

Howard: What's that?

Thomas: Mr. Flight Lieutenant Rawlings and his PNDC.*

*On December 31, 1981, Flight Lieutenant Jerry Rawlings, along with a small group of soldiers, launched a successful coup against the Ghanian government. Rawlings became Chairman of the Provisional National Defense Council (PNDC), the Ghanian ruling council.

Howard: Mr. Okono has managed to work well with all the regimes.

Thomas: But Rawlings is different. He's dedicated himself to ferreting out corruption and black marketeers. If Okono were caught, why the whole future of Wilson would be in danger in West Africa. Can't you just see how tidy it would be for the new government to discover that a foreign company was bribing his government administrators?

Teele: That's a point. But when Rawlings was in power before, there were no major crackdowns. Besides, every regime claims to be in favor of "cleaning up" the country, but it rarely seems to happen.

Howard: Still, Ian has a point. Though I'm no expert, Mr. Rawlings does seem quite intent on this policy.

Teele: I feel all this talk of external matters has not gotten us very far. What do we do about Mr. Okono? I really can't see firing him without at least getting an explanation from him.

EXHIBITS AND SUPPORTING MATERIALS

Exhibit 1. Cover Letter from Sylvia Appleby, Accountant for Firmin and Goodheart, Accompanying Her Financial Report on Wilson Chemicals (Ghana) Ltd.

Firmin and Goodheart
Certified Public Accountants
67 Grange St.
London, EC3, England
Telephone 01 424-0670

12 February, 1984

Mr. Ian Thomas
Director, West African Division
Wilson Chemicals
74, The Oaks
London, WC2

Dear Mr. Thomas:

Enclosed is the financial report of your subsidiary, Wilson Chemicals (Ghana) Ltd. During the audit made by our Accra office at your request several discrepancies were reported. Some of the errors were

---

procedural; others, I'm afraid, were more serious. Specifically, I refer to approximately £50,000 which were unaccounted for by the financial officer, Mr. G. Johnson. When queried by our auditors, Mr. Johnson replied that the money had been spent by Mr. Okono and his executives as ''incentives'' to increase or maintain business. There did not seem to be any attempt to cover this expense; however, Mr. Johnson noted that in the past these ''incentives'' had been written off as sales promotion costs.

In light of these findings, we find it impossible to certify your subsidiary as financially in conformance with accepted accounting practices. Please contact me if you have any further questions regarding this matter.

Very truly yours,

Sylvia Appleby

Sylvia Appleby

SA:bf
Enclosures

Exhibit 2. Letter from Okono to Howard

Wilson Chemicals (Ghana) Ltd.

P.O. Box 272   Accra, Ghana

20 February, 1984

Mr. George Howard
President
Wilson Chemicals
74, The Oaks
London, WC2, England

Dear Mr. Howard,

Your letter of 13 February arrived here today. Your concerns are justified, but things are not (exactly) as they seem.

You accuse me of bribery. I do not deny it. Indeed, some £47,000 were expended last year, a year of some chaos may I remind you, in an effort to maintain sales. I assure you that this money was spent solely for this purpose; neither I nor any other Wilson executives profited personally from this outlay.

The economic situation here in Ghana is not good. Last year was a year of drought. Food production dropped. Cocoa, the main crop of Ghana, declined to 110,000 tons, the lowest yield since the 1920s. And yet, Mr. Howard, Wilson's sales of chemical fertilizers did not decline. Fuel shortages are acute. We have, however, had enough fuel to continue operations at a normal level. Other companies have failed. The Ministry of Industries has halted or made difficult the importation of machinery. Some companies wait months for needed goods to clear customs. Our goods are cleared in days.

Why have we been successful when others have not? The answer lies in an outlay of £47,000 as incentives to individuals to give Wilson ''extra consideration''. Of course, this practice is undesirable, yet, it has been necessary to preserve business—your business, my business.

In your letter you state concern about the Rawlings government. I too am concerned, yet not because I fear interference in the practice of rewarding incentives to key administrators. I, probably more than anyone else, would be delighted if ''corruption'' were ended, if business could proceed without the need for inducements. What concerns me about Mr. Rawlings is his anti-business stand. This is far more worrisome than his ''crackdown'' on corruption, as this stance could really imperil Wilson.

Since Rawlings and the PNDC took power again at the end of 1981, there has, however, been little change in the way business has been conducted. In fact, we have made great efforts to work with the government, and I see no reason why this should change. The truth is, Ghana needs Wilson. Wilson also needs Ghana. It is a give-and-take relationship. Our goal, as is yours, is not to damage this relationship. Mr. Howard, trust me. For the last thirteen years I have made Wilson work, and work well. I see no reason to believe I cannot continue to do so, but I must be able to have a free hand (as I have had). Wilson will not fail in Ghana as long as I am allowed to direct the subsidiary's policies as I see fit.

I remain,

loyally yours,

Joseph Okono

Joseph Okono

Exhibit 3. Gross Sales, Wilson Chemicals (Ghana) Ltd., 1973–1983 (In Thousands of Pounds Sterling)

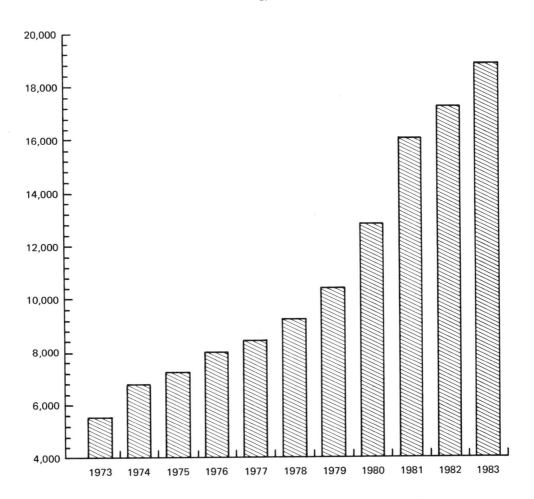

Exhibit 4. Brief Summary of the Rawlings Government Crackdown on Public Corruption*

In 1982, Mr. K. Edusei, a former leading member of the now banned People's National Party, was imprisoned for accepting £5,000 from an Italian businessman.

*Source: The Economist Intelligence Unit, *Quarterly Economic Review of Ghana, Sierra Leone, Gambia, and Liberia*, No. 4, 1983, p. 9.

In 1983 the crackdown continued:

A number of civil servants were dismissed on charges of corruption or embezzling.

Nine senior police officials and fifteen others were retired early for alleged profiteering.

The Director of Prisons and other senior prison officials were dismissed for a variety of reasons.

Some officials of the Ghana Water and Sewage Corporation, the Ghana National Trading Corporation, and the Cocoa Marketing Board have been ordered to stand trial for tax evasion.

Sixty-nine officials, including sixteen principal and assistant principal secretaries, have been forced to quit the Foreign Affairs Ministry for financial irregularities.

Some Points to Keep in Mind

Bribery for profit is an old and widespread practice. From the Persian Gulf to the Far East, from Latin America to Africa, an extraordinary amount of money is paid by corporations for the purposes of securing a contract, increasing or maintaining business, or avoiding bureaucratic red tape. Although generally frowned upon, payoffs for profit show no signs of disappearing.

Some efforts have been made to curb bribery. Following the Lockheed scandal of the mid-1970s in which the Lockheed Corporation was found guilty of bribing Japanese industrial and government officials, the United States passed the U.S. Foreign Corrupt Practices Act. This 1977 law made it a criminal offense for U.S. companies to pay bribes abroad. Many countries, however, have done little, if anything, to curb the practice. Most Western European countries, for instance, either openly approve bribery or ignore it. Italy, for example, passed a law in 1980 making it legal for Italian companies to use bribery for obtaining foreign business. France has no laws governing payoffs; West Germany and Great Britain have only weak legislation.

In this case it is clear that bribery, while not encouraged by the parent company, is acknowledged as a reality. Okono, in fact, argues that it is a necessity and that it is directly responsible for the high profits of the subsidiary. In the end the problem becomes more complex, but it basically hinges on the question, should a company put morality above profits?

CHECKLIST AND WORKSHEET

In coming to a decision about this case, did you consider the following?

The obvious illegality of Okono's dealings

The differing attitudes of the directors

Okono's defense

The financial rewards supposedly gained from bribery

The moral consequences

The possible business consequences of continuing/not continuing the practice

The crackdown on corruption by the Rawlings government

What other factors should be considered?

_____

_____

_____

_____

Decision:

_____

_____

_____

_____

DISCUSSION QUESTIONS

I. Background and Dialogue
1. What are the reasons for Wilson's success? How has Okono contributed to that success?
2. How would you characterize the basic position of Thomas regarding Okono? Of Teele? Of Howard?

3. What does Howard mean when he says, "We were more interested in the end than in the means"? How does this relate to the central problem in the case?
4. Why does Thomas feel that the future of Wilson in West Africa could be in danger?

II. Exhibits and Supporting Materials
   1. What is the significance of the following sentence from Exhibit 1?

> There did not seem to be any attempt to cover this expense; however, Mr. Johnson noted that in the past these "incentives" had been written off as sales promotion costs.

   2. Summarize Okono's letter (Exhibit 2). Why does he feel justified in bribing officials? How would you characterize his attitude? Apologetic? Arrogant? Self-confident?
   3. What does Exhibit 3 demonstrate? How is it related to the controversy?
   4. Does Exhibit 4 contradict or support Thomas's concerns? How?

EXERCISES

I. In the exercise below, read over the sentences taken from the case. Using the contextual clues, choose the best definition for the italicized word.
   1. Mr. Okono has *a free hand* to distribute gratuities to whomever he desires.
      a. hold
      b. freedom
      c. maneuverability
   2. He's dedicated himself to *ferreting out* corruption and black marketeers. If Okono were caught, the whole future of Wilson would be in danger in West Africa.
      a. helping
      b. freeing
      c. finding
   3. When Rawlings was in power before, there were no major *crackdowns*. Besides, every regime claims to be in favor of "cleaning up" the country.
      a. break-ups
      b. enforcing of the laws
      c. struggles

4. During the audit several *discrepancies* were reported. Some of the errors were procedural; others, I'm afraid, were more serious.
   a. charges
   b. opinions
   c. unexplained differences

5. When *queried* by our auditors, Mr. Johnson replied that the money had been spent as "incentives."
   a. asked
   b. remarked
   c. quarreled with

6. Indeed, some £47,000 were *expended* last year. I assure you that this money was spent solely to maintain sales.
   a. acquired
   b. bought
   c. used

7. Although generally *frowned upon,* payoffs for profit show no signs of disappearing.
   a. disapproved of
   b. thought highly of
   c. encouraged

8. Many countries have done little, if anything, to *curb* the practice. Most Western European countries, for instance, either openly approve bribery or ignore it.
   a. encourage
   b. endorse
   c. stop

9. In the end, the problem becomes more complex, but it basically *hinges* on the question, Should a company put morality above profits?
   a. answers
   b. functions
   c. turns

10. Mr. Okono must be fired. We cannot allow this situation to *endure* any longer than it has.
    a. ensure
    b. go on
    c. confuse

II. The Background contains information both about the Ghanian subsidiary and Mr. Okono. Rewrite the Background so that it describes Mr. Okono in relation to the company instead of the company in relation to Mr. Okono. Use the information from the Background to help you.

Mr. Joseph Okono _____

_____

An Oxford-educated Ghanian, _____

_____

He had increased sales _____

In addition, _____

_____

_____

A careful examination _____

_____

It appeared that _____

_____

This money had chiefly _____

_____

III. Write a response to Okono's letter (Exhibit 2). Base your response both on your personal views and on the facts presented in the case. You might want to consider the following:

Were bribes really necessary to ensure business success?

How important is the Rawlings government's attitude toward corruption?

What part of the total sales is £47,000?

What is the role of the parent company in dictating policy at the subsidiary level?

IV. Write a paragraph describing the sales trends over the past five years. Use the information from Exhibit 3.

V. Write a brief report expanding the information in Exhibit 1. Here are some additional facts:

1. Sales promotion costs were poorly documented. Only broad categories such as advertising and marketing were used to document expenses.
2. Travel allowances were not recorded correctly. There was no record of how much any individual was paid for any trip, and over one third of the receipts were missing. Travel allowances for the year totaled, when converted to pounds sterling, £8,321.
3. Expense accounts were also poorly documented. Mr. Okono's account alone had receipts for only £1,874, yet he was allocated £6,000.
4. The bank statements show withdrawals, presumably by Mr. Johnson, of £485 and £575 in February and June, respectively. These are not accounted for in the books.

VI. Expand the dialogue between Thomas, Teele, and Howard (after they have received Okono's letter).

Thomas: Although I must admit that Okono's letter is eloquent, it doesn't change a thing.

Howard: _____

_____

Teele: Gerald's got a point. It's impossible to ignore that things certainly have gone very smoothly there.

Thomas: _____

_____

Howard: I realize that it's still dishonest, but is it right to judge Okono by British standards?

Thomas: _____

_____

Teele: Yes, that's true. But as Gerald pointed out, Ghana is not England.

Thomas: _____

_____

VII. Perform the following guided role plays. (See Case 1 Exercises for instructions.)
   1. Okono is talking with Howard, Teele, and Thomas in London, explaining further the missing £47,000.
   2. Okono and Johnson are meeting to discuss the best strategy for dealing with the parent company's concern.
   3. Howard and Teele are meeting to discuss the situation. They are as concerned about Mr. Thomas's attitude as about the apparent bribery.

VIII. Debate one of the following issues. (See Case 1 Exercises for instructions.)
   1. Does a foreign country have a right to impose its standards on the host country?
   2. Is Okono justified in using bribes to gain business?
   3. Is the West to blame for the situation of bribery around the world?

IX. Write an analysis of the case from the point of view of either Okono, Thomas, or Howard.

3 Millars Bank Ltd.

BACKGROUND

Mr. P. D. Smothers, manager of Millars Bank Ltd. in Abu Dhabi, the United Arab Emirates, paced the floor of his stately office. Looking out the large window across the busy modern city, he contemplated his next move regarding his newly arrived corporate loan officer, J. L. Marsh, *Ms.* J. L. Marsh.

Ms. Marsh had come highly recommended. She had been in corporate banking for twelve years, the last ten in Beirut and Cairo, spoke Arabic fluently, and had been credited with arranging a number of highly complex, yet extremely successful loans in her former position. But last week she had been assigned to his office, and in the United Arab Emirates women did not hold such positions.

Smothers had at first been delighted. The head office in England had telexed the news that it had found a suitable replacement for the former loan officer and had included a brief account of Ms. Marsh, an account that surpassed his expectations. But, in typical telex fashion, the head office had only used initials: J. L. Marsh. The last thing he expected was that J. L. would turn out to be Janet Louise.

DIALOGUE: THE RIGHT PERSON FOR THE JOB?

CAST: P. D. Smothers, bank manager, Millars Bank, Abu Dhabi

Janet Marsh, new loan officer, Millars Bank, Abu Dhabi

Mr. Smothers and Ms. Marsh are meeting in Mr. Smothers's office in Abu Dhabi.

Smothers:	Miss Marsh, I frankly don't know what to say. I would have thought, with your obvious knowledge of the Middle East, that you would have disqualified yourself from this position.
Marsh:	Mr. Smothers, I understand what you're trying to tell me, but I really don't see that we have a problem. Believe it or not, when I was first transferred to Cairo five years ago, John, John Phillips, the manager there, had very much the same reservations you have today.
Smothers:	I know John. Know him very well.
Marsh:	Well, it worked out beautifully.
Smothers:	But, Egypt is *not* Abu Dhabi. Egypt is progressive, very liberal, women are acknowledged as professionals. But in the Emirates . . .
Marsh:	You don't want me to stay.
Smothers:	It's not me. Please understand that I would be delighted to have you stay. But, but, I can't imagine, Miss Marsh, how you could do your job. Our clients are conservative, traditional. They expect their principal loan officer to be a man. They won't do business with us. They won't take us seriously.
Marsh:	Why not?
Smothers:	They just won't. It's simply not done. Unheard of, even.
Marsh:	With all due respect, I think you're vastly mistaken.
Smothers:	What?
Marsh:	That's right. Mistaken. Our clients come to our bank to borrow pounds in order to finance projects that must be paid in pounds. Nothing more, nothing less. What they are looking for is a loan officer who can place their loan at a competitive interest rate and in short order. Isn't that correct?
Smothers:	Yes. And no.
Marsh:	Why no?
Smothers:	Miss Marsh, you've been in corporate banking long enough to realize that personal relations between a client and a lending institution are vitally important. I, I can't see how our clients could, would relate to you. And we're not the only bank in town either. Why, just in Abu Dhabi alone there are at least two dozen foreign banks with whom we are in direct competition, not to mention the other two dozen Emirate-owned banks plus all the other foreign banks with representatives on restricted licenses who also can occasionally take business away from us.
Marsh:	Mr. Smothers, I am well aware of competition and the role of the loan officer. I am so well aware, in fact, that I feel that I can be as effective or more effective than I was in Beirut and

Cairo. I understand the Middle East. I've lived here for many years. I speak, read, and write Arabic. I know the customs, the religion, the history, and, most importantly, the business of business. How many other loan officers are fluent in Arabic?

Smothers: Not many. I'm not even myself. But that has not been a disadvantage.

Marsh: Has it been an advantage?

Smothers: No, I can't say that either.

Marsh: Besides, Mr. Smothers, let me remind you that this is a British bank, not an Arab bank and . . .

Smothers: But a British bank in an Arab country.

EXHIBITS AND SUPPORTING MATERIALS

Exhibit I. Telex from W. T. R. Duncan, Vice-President, International Banking, Millars Bank, London, to Smothers

```
LND BUS     18 Jul 1984


TO:  P. SMOTHERS

FM:  W. DUNCAN

RE:  REPLACEMENT OFFICER


J. L. MARSH, REPLACEMENT FOR MATHERS, ARRIVING 1 AUG FOR ASSIGNMENT 15

AUG. MARSH FORMERLY CORPORATE LOAN OFFICER, BEIRUT AND CAIRO. FLUENT

ARABIC. HIGHLY SUCCESSFUL IN FORMER POSITIONS. CREDITED WITH

EXPANDING CAIRO LOAN OPERATIONS BY 30%. SHOULD BE ABLE TO ASSUME

EXTENSIVE DUTIES IN MIN. TIME. PLS REPLY UPON MARSH ARRIVAL.


CORDIALLY,

DUNCAN
```

Exhibit 2. Résumé of Janet Marsh

Janet Louise Marsh   Health: Excellent
c/o Millars Bank   Citizenship: United Kingdom
14 Talaat Harb St.   Marital Status: Single
Cairo, Egypt   Date of Birth: 4 Jan., 1951

Employment History:

11/78 to present   Millars Bank (Cairo) Ltd.
                        14 Talaat Harb St., Cairo, Egypt
                        Position: Corporate Loan Officer
                        Duties:

                        Liaison with clients; Processing of
                        acceptances and transit items; financial
                        investigations; Eurodollar financing;
                        project evaluations.

                        Supervisor: John R. Phillips

6/75 to 11/78   Millars Bank (Beirut) Ltd.
                        POB 1028, Beirut, Lebanon
                        Position: Assistant Corporate Loan Officer
                        Duties:

                        Processing of acceptances and transit items;
                        financial investigations; liaison with
                        clients.

9/72 to 6/75   Millars Bank, International Division
                        58 Lombard St., London EC3, England
                        Position: Assistant, International Finance
                        Duties:

                        Processing of letters of credit, acceptances,
                        and transit items; Eurodollar loan financing;
                        Middle East finance specialist. Translator
                        and interpreter: Arabic–English, English–
                        Arabic.

Education:

                        London School of Economics
                        Houghton St., London WC2A 2PE, England

                        B.Sc. (Econ) June 1972
                        Programme: Monetary Economics

                        Major Studies: Monetary Economics, Finance,
                        Accounting, Arabic, International Finance

```
Publications:
                     ''The Changing Character of International
                     Finance in Egypt,'' Banking International,
                     v. 14, no. 63, 1982.

Languages:

                     Arabic, French (fluent)
                     German (reading knowledge)

Leisure Activities:

                     Tennis, Swimming, Photography
```

Exhibit 3. Texts of a Series of Telexes Sent Back and Forth from Smothers to Duncan

Telex from Smothers to Duncan:

> JANET MARSH ARRIVED YESTERDAY. HAVE SERIOUS DOUBTS AS TO HER ABILITY TO
> PERFORM DUTIES ADEQUATELY GIVEN STRONG TRAD ARAB CULTURE HERE. PLEASE
> ADVISE ASAP.

Telex from Duncan to Smothers:

> PLS CLARIFY MESSAGE RE MARSH.

Telex from Smothers to Duncan:

> CLARIFICATION REGARDING JANET MARSH: FEEL ARABS WILL NOT DEAL WITH
> WOMAN LOAN OFFICER. EMIRATES VERY TRADITIONAL, NOT ACCUSTOMED TO
> FEMALES IN BUS. COULD SERIOUSLY JEOPARDIZE OPERATIONS. PLS ADVISE.

Exhibit 4. Letter from Marsh to Smothers

Dear Mr. Smothers:

In relation to our conversation of yesterday, I feel some further clarification of my position is desirable.

Let me assure you, first, that I did not apply for this position in order to create a ''test'' case regarding the employment of women in executive positions in the Arab world. It is simply that the qualifications posted for the position were ideally suited to my talents.

Let me also assure you that I gave considerable thought to the possible complications involved, but felt, and still feel, that my own administrative skills are sufficient to overcome objections that might arise initially from our predominantly Arab clientele. My positions in both Beirut and Cairo have taught me much about how to proceed in the Middle East, and I trust I can draw on those lessons to ensure a smooth and speedy transition from Cairo to Abu Dhabi.

In Cairo I worked with a number of Saudi clients and, in general, had friendly and excellent relationships with them. Although they were certainly traditional in their social views, I found them to be extremely progressive in their business outlook. This progressive viewpoint extended to our client/banker relationship, where I was simply seen as ''a banker''. Their attitude was quite clearly one of financial pragmatism, i.e., if Millars employed me in such a position, I must be qualified.

Additional anecdotes abound; however, in most of them ''financial pragmatism'' was more important than ''cultural tradition''. Had I been an Arab woman, things might have been different, but as an Englishwoman working for an English bank, I have been allowed to stand outside the ''cultural tradition''.

In conclusion, Mr. Smothers, I simply urge you to grant me the opportunity to serve Millars Bank in Abu Dhabi. If my performance is not satisfactory, I promise to step down from the position within ninety days.

I thank you in advance for your consideration.

Very truly yours,

J. L. Marsh

J. L. Marsh

2 Aug., 1984

Some Points to Keep in Mind

The position of women in Arab societies, contrary to many assumptions, is in a state of evolution. This evolution, however, is at various stages. In Egypt, Lebanon, Syria, and Jordan, for instance, traditional views that women are second to men have largely disappeared. Opportunities for higher education and professional careers in such traditionally "male" occupations as engineering, science, and medicine are now open to women in these countries, as well as in many other parts of the Middle East and North Africa.

The situation in this case is in some sense a clash of cultures between not only the West and the Middle East, but also between traditional and modern Arab societies. The Arabian Peninsula, for example, is the most conservative region in the area, with women rarely holding important positions. Given this fact, the central question then really becomes one of whether or not, in the name of "progress," it is right to impose one's own values on another culture. In other words, since Abu Dhabi is the host country to Millars Bank, does the bank have an obligation to conform to the customs of the country or to uphold its own "tradition" of granting equal opportunity to women? On a business level does it make sense to do so? Finally, can the positive experience of Ms. Marsh in "Westernized" countries like Lebanon and Egypt be applied to the situation in Abu Dhabi?

CHECKLIST AND WORKSHEET

In coming to a decision about this case, did you consider the following?

  Marsh's qualifications and past history in the Middle East

  Smothers's position

  The conservative tradition and attitudes of the United Arab Emirates

  Marsh's position that "business is business"

  The possible financial consequences to Millars Bank resulting from employing Marsh in Abu Dhabi

What other factors should be considered?

_____

_____

_____

Decision:

_____

_____

_____

_____

DISCUSSION QUESTIONS

   I. Background and Dialogue
1. Why had Smothers not known that his new loan officer was a woman? Why does he feel that it is a problem?
2. Why does Smothers feel Marsh should have disqualified herself from taking the position?
3. Why does Marsh feel confident that she'll be able to do the job? What are her past achievements?
4. How is the central issue in the case tied to the fact that Millars Bank is a "British bank in an Arab country"?

   II. Exhibits and Supporting Materials
1. What significant fact is missing from the description of Marsh in Exhibit 1? Should it have been included or should it matter? Why do you think Smothers assumed that J. L. Marsh was a man?
2. Summarize Marsh's professional career as revealed in Exhibit 2. Has she advanced quickly? How have her duties changed from one job to the next?
3. Analyze the series of telexes in Exhibit 3. Why does Smothers initially telex Duncan? Why doesn't Duncan understand?
4. Why does Marsh write Smothers a letter (Exhibit 4)? What is her new proposal? How would you characterize the tone of the letter?

EXERCISES

I. Dictionaries often give several definitions for one word. To decide which meaning is correct, you must look carefully at the context in which the unfamiliar word occurs. In the exercise below, select from among the three correct meanings of the italicized word the definition that best defines the word as it is used in the sentence. All of the sentences are drawn from the case.

1. Mr. P. D. Smothers *paced* the floor of his stately office.
   a. a single step, or its distance
   b. walked back and forth
   c. walked at a certain rate

2. He *contemplated* his next move regarding his newly arrived corporate loan officer.
   a. expected
   b. meditated
   c. reflected upon attentively

3. She had been *credited* with arranging a number of highly complex, yet extremely successful loans.
   a. believed
   b. favorably acknowledged
   c. had a payment deposited in her account

4. When I was first assigned to Cairo, the manager there had very much the same *reservations* you have today.
   a. the act of keeping back or withholding
   b. a tract of public land set aside for some special use
   c. concerns about going ahead with a plan

5. They expect their *principal* loan officer to be a man.
   a. the head of a school
   b. first in rank or importance
   c. employer of an agent

6. Duties: Processing of *acceptances* and transit items.
   a. approvals
   b. the acts of accepting
   c. bills one has agreed to pay later

7. She should be able to *assume* extensive duties in minimum time.
   a. take for granted without proof
   b. pretend to possess
   c. take upon oneself; undertake

8. I urge you to *grant* me the opportunity to serve Millars Bank.
   a. give; bestow upon someone
   b. convey by deed
   c. to concede to be true

9. I thank you in advance for your *consideration.*
   a. a careful reflection
   b. thoughtfulness of others
   c. motive; reason
10. Can the positive experience of Ms. Marsh in "Westernized" countries be *applied* to the situation in Abu Dhabi?
    a. devoted to a particular purpose
    b. laid on
    c. put to use

II. The first paragraph in the Background describes Mr. Smothers's actions and thoughts. Reread the paragraph; then write a paragraph of the same sort describing Ms. Marsh's actions and thoughts before meeting with Mr. Smothers. Use information from the Dialogue and the exhibits to help you.

III. A telex uses many abbreviations and frequently omits many parts of speech (verbs, prepositions, articles). Rewrite the telexes in Exhibits 1 and 3 so that they are in complete sentences.

IV. Continue the dialogue between Marsh and Smothers (after Mr. Smothers has received Ms. Marsh's letter).

Smothers: Ms. Marsh, I got your letter and have read it over very carefully.

Marsh: _____
          _____

Smothers: Well, I don't quite know what to think.

Marsh: _____
          _____

Smothers: I guess what I'm trying to say, is that although you make a number of good points, I'm not sure they change the situation.

Marsh: _____
          _____

Smothers: Yes, that's true. The ninety-day trial period is a new idea.

Marsh: _____

_____

Smothers: Well, I'd like to consider it some more. I'm just worried that it wouldn't be fair to you. I mean, in ninety days you'd just be getting used to the job and if . . .

Marsh: _____

_____

Smothers: Yes, I suppose that's true. It might work out fine. But, if it doesn't, it would be very difficult for both of us.

Marsh: _____

_____

V. Write a memo from Smothers to his staff introducing Ms. Marsh. Use the information from the résumé (Exhibit 2) and from the other parts of the case. Make sure you give some details about her previous positions as well as information about her new job.

VI. Ms. Marsh began this letter to a friend after her arrival in Abu Dhabi. Finish the letter by drawing on the information from the case.

> I finally have arrived in Abu Dhabi. I was surprised by the modernness of the city—indeed, it seems as if all the buildings are new. I have already found a number of shops that look like they'll be fun to browse in. Don't worry about me missing anything for a comfortable life. They have everything here, even English marmalade! Next week I'll look for an apartment.
>
> The only problem, so far, is that I don't know how long I'll be able to stay. The boss at the bank, Mr. Smothers, doesn't think it will work out for me here. Why? Because I'm a woman, and he feels that I won't be able to deal effectively with the Arab clients. Yesterday we had a long talk and . . .

VII. Perform the following guided role plays. (See Case 1 Exercises for instructions.)
   1. Janet Marsh is talking with Smothers in the following situations:

a. upon arrival in Abu Dhabi
b. after her first week on the job
c. after three months on the job

2. Marsh is meeting with an influential Abu Dhabi businessman who wishes to arrange a loan for £4 million for payment to a British construction firm.

3. Smothers is talking on the phone with W. T. R. Duncan, Vice-President, International Banking, in London.

VIII. Debate one of the following topics. (See Case 1 Exercises for instructions.)

1. A business should place its business above moral issues, particularly when profits are at stake.

2. Equality for women should be a given. The only way in which complete equality will come about is if women are given positions of authority that they have earned.

IX. Write an analysis of the case from the point of view of either Marsh or Smothers.

4 Leclerc Machines de Cuisine

BACKGROUND

Leclerc Machines de Cuisine, a Paris manufacturer of food processors, blenders, grinders, and other chef's supplies, had recently begun exporting its products to the United States through a sole U.S. distributor, Creative Cuisines, Inc., an Atlanta, Georgia, firm. Although at first reluctant to accept an exclusive distribution agreement, Leclerc had finally been persuaded to do so when Creative Cuisines agreed to assume all marketing and sales promotion costs for the Leclerc line and had further agreed to market the products aggressively.

It was quite a surprise then when in July 1984 Creative Cuisines learned that someone else in the U.S., a mail order firm calling itself Reliable Restaurant and Home Kitchen Supplies, began to place ads in consumer magazines and trade journals offering the Leclerc LMC Professional and the Leclerc LMC Standard food processors at prices considerably lower than those offered by Creative Cuisines.

The president of Creative Cuisines, Mr. Bill Lewis, immediately called Leclerc when he learned of the ads to see if somehow Leclerc was responsible. Leclerc's overseas sales manager, Mr. François Jost, said that Leclerc had not authorized a sale to Reliable and expressed his dismay that Reliable had managed to receive shipments. Mr. Lewis then proceeded to investigate Reliable, but with little success. He learned only that they were a New Jersey company specializing in mail order discount kitchen supplies. His next step was to consult his firm's attorney, Marie Dominic, to determine what legal action could be taken.

DIALOGUE: A PARALLEL IMPORT PROBLEM

CAST: Mr. Bill Lewis, President, Creative Cuisines, Inc.

Ms. Marie Dominic, attorney representing Creative Cuisines

Mr. Lewis and Ms. Dominic are meeting in Ms. Dominic's office to discuss possible legal action against Reliable Restaurant and Home Kitchen Supplies.

Dominic: From what you told me on the phone, Bill, this sounds like a clear-cut case of parallel import.

Lewis: Is that legal?

Dominic: It depends on how Reliable is getting the Leclerc products.

Lewis: What do you mean?

Dominic: If Reliable is getting its products direct from Leclerc in violation of your exclusive distribution agreement, it's illegal. Or, it's illegal if the Leclerc products it's selling are counterfeits, not genuine Leclerc products.

Lewis: Well, Leclerc claims to have no knowledge of the shipments.

Dominic: Are the products genuine?

Lewis: They seem to be. We're getting one this week, and believe me, we'll take the thing apart if we have to in order to determine whether it's genuine.

Dominic: Okay, that's a good step. If they aren't genuine, you both—Leclerc and you—have a case.

Lewis: My feeling, though, is that they really are Leclerc products. They're offering a manufacturer's warranty. Hey, that's illegal isn't it?

Dominic: Not necessarily.

Lewis: What?

Dominic: Well, if Reliable is offering a manufacturer's warranty, then Leclerc has to honor it. As long as the goods are legitimate.

Lewis: But we're the only authorized service center in the U.S.

Dominic: True, but Reliable could send the food processors directly to Leclerc or to the distributor from whom they purchased the products.

Lewis: I don't know about that. On the warranty the return card is printed with our address. We maintain all of that information here.

Dominic: They might have had their own warranty cards printed, or there is a possibility that they could just have all the service

	done by you. Do you know all of the customers who bought your supplies?
Lewis:	No. But we can institute a careful check. Also, I'm sure that there's some way to find out who actually bought C.C.-supplied processors.
Dominic:	What are we talking about in terms of loss in sales revenue?
Lewis:	Well, I don't know what Reliable's sales are. But our sales are off about 30 percent this month.
Dominic:	Is that unusual for July?
Lewis:	Not in general. But I don't know with this product. We only started distributing it in January. Our forecast calls for a steady increase in sales. But that's beside the point. What can we legally do to stop these pirates?
Dominic:	First, I'll write a letter to Reliable implying possible illegalities. Meanwhile, you see what you can find out about Reliable's source of supply. Get Leclerc to issue a warning to its foreign distributors. Most likely one of its own distributors, maybe in Canada or in Europe, is supplying Reliable with products. That happens quite often. In many cases the distributor doesn't even know he's violating an agreement. The truth is, though, these measures may be ineffective. I suggest you immediately adopt some marketing tactics to counter this offensive—the same way you would with any other competitive threat.

EXHIBITS AND SUPPORTING MATERIALS

Exhibit I. Letter from Dominic to Albert Rose, President, Reliable Restaurant and Home Kitchen Supplies

---

Owens, Garfield and Sutton, Inc.
Attorneys at Law
6475 Macon Place, Suite 602
Atlanta, Georgia 02466
(404)646-8259

July 31, 1984

Mr. Albert Rose, President
Reliable Restaurant and Home Kitchen Supplies
Box 406
Newark, NJ 02041

Dear Mr. Rose:

My client, Creative Cuisines, Inc., has recently brought to my attention that you have either knowingly or unknowingly violated the exclusive distribution agreement between Leclerc Machines de Cuisine and Creative Cuisines, Inc. This agreement, which went into effect in January of this year, explicitly gives sole distribution rights to Creative Cuisines and also names them as the only authorized service agent of Leclerc in the U.S.A.

Your distribution of Leclerc products is a grievous violation of this agreement. Full legal proceedings shall be brought to bear against you unless you desist, at once, in acting as an alternative source of supply for Leclerc products in the U.S.

Thank you for your prompt attention to this matter.

Very truly yours,

Marie Dominic

Marie Dominic, Esq.

Exhibit 2. Reliable's Ad in a Number of Consumer Food Magazines and
Professional Journals

SAVE 30%
off
List Price!!

FULL
Factory
Warranty!!

Get The Best. Get A Leclerc Food Processor.
Professional Model ONLY $319 (1 Gal. Capacity, 6
blades); Standard Model ONLY $189 (½ Gal. Capacity,
4 blades). That's a savings of 30% off the List Price.
Better yet, you don't even have to leave your kitchen.
Just clip the coupon below or call our toll free number
today:

1-800-555-5342

MC, VISA, AMEX, DINERS CLUB accepted

_____

YES, I want a Leclerc Food Processor

Name _____

Address _____

_____

_____

Model: Standard $189 _____   QTY _____

           Professional $319 _____   QTY _____

Amt. Enclosed   (please add an additional $6 for
                          postage and handling)
$_____

Charge Me: Card Type _____ # _____

Exhibit 3. English Version of a Letter Sent by Leclerc to All Distributors

---

Leclerc Machines de Cuisine
145, bd. Richard-Lenoir
75011 Paris
Tel (1) 805. 48. 22
Telex 270848

ATTENTION ALL DISTRIBUTORS:

    Recently our exclusive U.S. distributor, Creative Cuisines, Inc., discovered that another U.S. company, Reliable Restaurant and Home Kitchen Supplies, was selling Leclerc LMC Professional and LMC Standard food processors in the U.S. in violation of our agreement with Creative Cuisines.
    If by chance you have supplied Reliable Restaurant and Home Kitchen Supplies with these items, please do not do so in the future. This is a direct violation of our agreement with Creative Cuisines and cannot be tolerated.
    Thank you for your prompt action concerning this matter.

Exhibit 4. Memo from Jane Watson, Sales Manager, Creative Cuisines, to Bill Lewis

---

```
TO:    B. Lewis
FM:    J. Watson
RE:    Reliable Food Processor
DATE:  Aug. 4, 1984
```

The Leclerc Standard Food Processor was received today at my home and examined by me and our service staff here at the office. It is without a doubt a genuine Leclerc LMC Standard. The warranty, although identical to the one issued by Leclerc, France, names Reliable on the return card. I enclose it for your examination.

Exhibit 5. Memo to Creative Cuisines Sales Department from Jane Watson

---

CREATIVE CUISINES   *Jane Watson*

TO: Sales staff

RE: Price for Leclerc LMC food processors

Aug. 5, 1984

Effective immediately we are lowering the prices on the LMC

Professional Food Processor from $399 to $310 and on the LMC Standard

Food Processor from $279 to $189. This is a temporary two-month price

cut to head off illegal competition from Reliable. Please contact

dealers immediately to inform them of the savings. Ads, to be run in the

September issues of all magazines in which we are advertisers, will

reflect this change.

Exhibit 6. Letter to Bill Lewis from Sandra Jordan, Account Executive at
Feingold Advertising, Creative Cuisine's Advertising Agency

Feingold Advertising
1642 Ridgeway
Atlanta, Georgia
(404)621-0397

August 5, 1984

Dear Bill,

This is to confirm our conversation of this morning and provide some
immediate feedback regarding new ad copy and placement of ads in
September issues.

Concept: Aggressively take on Reliable. Ad should inform customers
             of Reliable's "pirate" actions. Emphasis will be placed on
             possibility that warranty will not be honored. Low price
             will also be advertised, but not focus. Standard graphics
             will be used.

Placement: I called all of the journals in which we advertise and
             alerted them that new copy would be arriving soon. We have
             until the 15th for <u>Gourmet</u>, <u>Boston Magazine</u>, and
             <u>Restaurant World</u>; until the 20th at the others.

Copy and Design: New copy and design will be ready for your approval
             tomorrow. We will meet at 3:00 P.M. as planned.
             Typesetting and mechanicals will take only 4–5 days
             so that negatives can be sent on, or about, the 12th
             of August.

We'll beat them at their own game. Good luck with the legal proceedings. Until tomorrow.

Cordially,

Sandra

Sandra

Some Points to Keep in Mind

Parallel import is defined as a situation in which identical products are imported by two different importers, but with only one importer having been granted the right by the manufacturer to do so. Although laws governing parallel import vary from country to country, it is usually seen as illegal only when the products are not genuine.

In this case Creative Cuisines has determined that Reliable's goods are genuine. If Leclerc has not directly exported the goods to the supplier, there is little legally that Creative Cuisines can do. The only defense Creative Cuisines has is to employ tactics to stop the competition while trying to get Leclerc to stop the flow of merchandise to Reliable. Although it is usually the best policy for the producers to halt the imports, the manufacturer often does little to stop the flow, rationalizing that "sales are sales" regardless of how they are made.

What must be decided then is the course of action that Creative Cuisines should take. While it is obvious that Creative Cuisines realizes how difficult it is to stop Reliable solely by legal means, is the strategy the firm is pursuing the best one? Is a more permanent lowering of prices or a different advertising strategy advisable? Of course, a more radical action is also possible: Creative Cuisines could stop acting as a distributor for Leclerc, either until the parallel import ceases or permanently.

CHECKLIST AND WORKSHEET

In coming to a decision about this case, did you consider the following?

The probable inability of Creative Cuisines to block Reliable's sales

The likely effect of Reliable's lower price on Creative Cuisines' sales

The long-term results of Creative Cuisines cutting its prices

The tactics used by Creative Cuisines to expose Reliable

Leclerc's position and actions

What other factors should be considered?

_____

_____

_____

_____

Decision:

_____

_____

_____

_____

DISCUSSION QUESTIONS

I. Background and Dialogue
1. Describe the relationship between Leclerc and Creative Cuisines.
2. Why was it such a surprise when Creative Cuisines learned that Reliable was also distributing the LMC food processors?
3. According to Dominic, in what situations would Reliable be violating the law?
4. Why does Dominic suggest that Creative Cuisines immediately adopt some new marketing strategies rather than wait for a legal investigation?

II. Exhibits and Supporting Materials
1. The letter in Exhibit 1 consists of two main paragraphs. What is the purpose of this structure? What does the first paragraph describe? The second?
2. Is the ad in Exhibit 2 informative, or does it rely on established knowledge about the LMC food processors? Why or why not?
3. Is the letter in Exhibit 3 persuasive? If yes, why? If not, how could it be made more so?
4. How do Exhibits 4, 5, and 6 connect with one another? What do these documents say about the situation? Given this strategy, does it seem as if Creative Cuisines believes it can legally stop Reliable? Support your answers with specific references to the exhibits.

EXERCISES

I. In the exercise below, read over the sentences drawn from the case. Using the contextual clues, choose the best definition for the italicized word.
1. Although at first *reluctant* to accept an exclusive distribution agreement, Leclerc had finally been persuaded to do so.
   a. happy
   b. eager
   c. unwilling
2. Mr. Jost said that Leclerc had not authorized a sale to Reliable and expressed his *dismay* that Reliable had managed to receive shipments.
   a. regret

   b. pleasure
   c. worries
3. His next step was to consult his firm's attorney to *determine* what legal action could be taken.
   a. understand
   b. deliver
   c. decide
4. It's illegal if the Leclerc products it's selling are *counterfeits,* not genuine Leclerc products.
   a. defective
   b. real
   c. fake
5. These measures may be ineffective. I suggest you adopt some marketing *tactics* to counter this offensive.
   a. strategies
   b. warnings
   c. decisions
6. You have violated the *exclusive* distribution agreement between Leclerc and Creative Cuisines. That agreement gives sole distribution rights to Creative Cuisines.
   a. snobbish
   b. inclusive
   c. shutting out all others
7. Full legal proceedings shall be brought against you unless you *desist,* at once, in acting as an alternative source of supply.
   a. consider
   b. speed up
   c. stop
8. I called all of the journals in which we advertise and *alerted* them that new copy will be arriving.
   a. warned
   b. supplied
   c. cautioned
9. The only defense Creative Cuisines has is to *employ* tactics to stop the flow of merchandise.
   a. give a job to
   b. give up
   c. use
10. Although it is usually the best policy for the producers to *halt* the imports, the manufacturer often does little to stop the flow.
    a. speed up
    b. slow down
    c. stop

II. There are only two sentences in the first paragraph of the Background. They are both compound sentences containing a number of coordinating conjunctions. Rewrite the first paragraph using simple sentences. The first few words of each sentence are supplied below for you.

1. Leclerc Machines de Cuisine _____

_____

2. They manufactured _____

_____

3. They had recently _____

_____

4. Their U.S. distributor _____

_____

5. Creative Cuisines _____

_____

6. Leclerc was _____

_____

7. They were finally persuaded _____

_____

8. Creative Cuisines agreed _____

_____

9. They further agreed _____

_____

III. Expand the dialogue between Dominic and Lewis.

Dominic: This sounds like a clear case of parallel import.

Lewis: _____

_____

Dominic: That's when identical products are imported by two different importers.

Lewis: _____

_____

Dominic: It depends on how Reliable is getting the products.

Lewis: _____

_____

Dominic: I know they aren't getting them from you, but are they getting them from Leclerc?

Lewis: _____

_____

Dominic: Well, then, are the products genuine?

Lewis: _____

_____

Dominic: When will you know for sure?

Lewis: _____

_____

IV. Write a business letter as Albert Rose, President of Reliable, answering Ms. Dominic's letter in Exhibit 1. As Rose, you will naturally want to defend your position quite strongly. Use information from the case to support your arguments.

V. Write an advertisement for Creative Cuisines in which you attempt to discredit Reliable and at the same time introduce the new price reduction on Leclerc food processors. Use the ideas in Exhibits 5 and 6 to help you.

VI. Look at the following chart of Creative Cuisines' sales over the last six months and write a summary of the trends. Make some assumptions about why sales fell in February and March; rose in April through June; and fell again in July.

Sales for Creative Cuisines of Food Processors (in thousands)

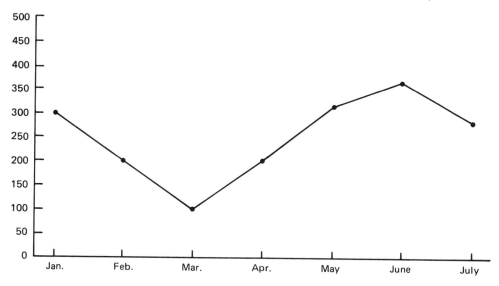

VII. Perform the following guided role plays. (See Case 1 Exercises for instructions.)

1. Lewis has just discovered that Reliable has been getting its products from a Canadian Leclerc distributor. He makes three phone calls:
   a. to Dominic
   b. to Jost (in France)
   c. to the Canadian distributor

2. Lewis is meeting with his staff to discuss the best strategy for combatting Reliable.

3. Jost is meeting with his staff to discuss the parallel import of Leclerc's food processors to the U.S.

VIII. Debate one of the following issues. (See Case 1 Exercises for instructions.)
1. Leclerc should not care how Reliable is getting Leclerc products since sales are sales.
2. Lewis is overreacting to the situation. He should simply try harder, lower his prices, and aggressively take on Reliable.

5 Tanaka Komuten Company, Ltd.

BACKGROUND

The Tanaka Komuten Company is a large Japanese general contractor noted for its excellence in the design and construction of office, commercial, and public buildings, multi-family housing, schools, and hotels. The family-owned company has grown rapidly since its founding in the 1930s, attaining a position as one of the top five construction firms in Japan, with 1982 sales in excess of US$2.3 billion. This success, in the opinion of the Tanaka family, was attributable to one main factor: the nondiversified character of the company.

This strategy of specialization proved quite effective during the 1950s, 1960s, and 1970s. The company easily gained building contracts, both domestically and internationally, and won numerous awards for its high quality of construction. In the 1980s, however, with the worldwide decline in building construction, Tanaka was finding itself for the first time in a rather precarious position.

It was clear that the old course of specialization was no longer as tenable as it had been. What direction Tanaka should pursue, though, was a matter of controversy within the company. The chairman of the board, Mr. Kazuo Tanaka, and his son, the president, Mr. Ruichi Tanaka, resisted expanding the Tanaka firm into other areas of construction. They had serious doubts as to whether Tanaka Komuten could actually compete with more established firms and feared that a move toward diversification would harm the reputation of excellence and dedication to building for which Tanaka was known. Most of the directors, however, felt that Tanaka Komuten should expand its civil engineering capacity, which presently accounted for less than 4 percent of its total sales.

The Tanakas resisted this idea, however, feeling that it would drain too many resources away from the main business activity and possibly even affect Tanaka's reputation as a dedicated general contractor. After months of discussion, but with no resolution of the dilemma, the position of the directors was strengthened by a new development: An offer was received from a former U.S. construction partner, Atlas Engineering & Construction, to form a joint venture company for the purpose of international civil engineering and building construction.

DIALOGUE: A JOINT VENTURE CONSIDERATION

CAST: Tom Jameson, President, Atlas Engineering & Construction

Kenji Taniguchi, Managing Director, Tanaka Komuten

Ruichi Tanaka, President, Tanaka Komuten

In the Osaka head office of Tanaka Komuten the American and Japanese executives are discussing the possibilities of forming a joint venture company.

Jameson: By now I'm sure you've had a chance to look over some of the documents I sent from Houston. I think it should be fairly clear that a joint venture for the purpose of obtaining worldwide contracts involving both civil and building engineering is a definite advantage for both of us.

Tanaka: There certainly are some positive aspects to your proposal. We still have some concerns, though.

Jameson: Of course. A number of details need to be ironed out, even explored further. What is your main concern?

Tanaka: Our main concern, to be perfectly honest, has little to do with the proposal itself. In fact, we find it rather sound. The problem is simply this: Tanaka Komuten has built a reputation on its commitment to design and building construction. We pride ourselves on this. It's what makes us different from our competitors.

Taniguchi: Yes. This policy is at the core of our business philosophy.

Jameson: I understand that. The fact of the matter, though, is this: By combining our respective strengths, we are not diminishing our own primary commitment either to building or civil engineering.

Taniguchi: In one way, that's true. In another, it isn't. By forming a separate company, we do maintain our primary enterprise as is. On the other hand, a major resource commitment, both in capital and in manpower, cannot help but affect Tanaka Komuten as a general contractor.

Jameson: But as I see it, we already are committed to that course. When we worked together in the Emirates, with you building the terminal and us the runways, we were doing just that. Also, I don't see that Tanaka Komuten will be changing its emphasis at all. You will still be in charge of design and building construction, Atlas in charge of civil engineering. What our joint venture company would do is simply make it easier to bid on projects.

Tanaka: That's a good point. It would definitely make it easier for prospective clients as well. The problem, though, is with our image. Will our existing clients see it that way, or will they feel that Tanaka Komuten has gone the way of all major contractors?

Jameson: If we make our relationship clear, do a little public relations work, I don't see any problem.

Taniguchi: It definitely bears consideration. There's obviously a lot to gain from a joint venture.

Jameson: And little risk, really. Also, since we will not do any joint venture work in Japan, your domestic clients will not be at all affected. And let's also face it, we need each other if we are to start increasing our growth. There's a lot of opportunity and revenue internationally. And with our collective experience and reputations, I really think we can turn this joint venture into a very profitable partnership.

EXHIBITS AND SUPPORTING MATERIALS

Exhibit 1. Summary of Main Points in Jameson's Proposal to Tanaka Komuten

Main Activities of the Joint Venture Company: To procure contracts internationally for projects involving both civil engineering and building construction, e.g., the design and construction of transportation facilities, rural factories requiring road and rail extensions, urban and regional planning and development, harbor facilities. In addition, the joint venture company would engage in activities related to these projects, such as material procurement, construction design and engineering (both civil and building), structural engineering, and land-use planning.

Purpose of the Joint Venture: To consolidate civil engineering and building construction capabilities in one single corporation. The immediate advantages of such a consolidation are:

1. Elimination of separate bid submission, thus reducing the cost factor involved in international feasibility study preparation.
2. Assurance to the client of integrated design, engineering, construction, and quality control.
3. Reduction in overall costs to the client.
4. Placement of Tanaka Komuten and Atlas Engineering in a competitive position in relation to other consolidated engineering and construction firms.

Investment Capital: Subject to negotiation and eventual scope of business. Probable minimum investment is US$500,000 each.

Equity: Equal participation, hence equal equity.

Distribution of Profit and Loss: Subject to negotiation and eventual structure of the company. On most projects, however, equal sharing is desirable. On some projects requiring additional resources provided by the respective parent companies, a percentage of invested capital, materials, and manpower resources will be returned/borne by the parent company.

Immediate Prospects for Joint Venture Bids:

Singapore: Marina City
              apartments and roads

Brazil: Pôrto Alegre–São Paulo
              rail and terminal improvements

Exhibit 2. Status of Projects Undertaken by Tanaka Komuten (In Billions of US$)

	Pending	*Contracted*	*Completed*
1980	2.416	2.352	2.320
1981	2.452	2.592	2.368
Net actual change, 1980–81	.036	.24	.048
Percent change, 1980–81	.015	.102	.0207

Exhibit 3. Ten-Year Growth Summary of Tanaka Komuten's Gross Sales

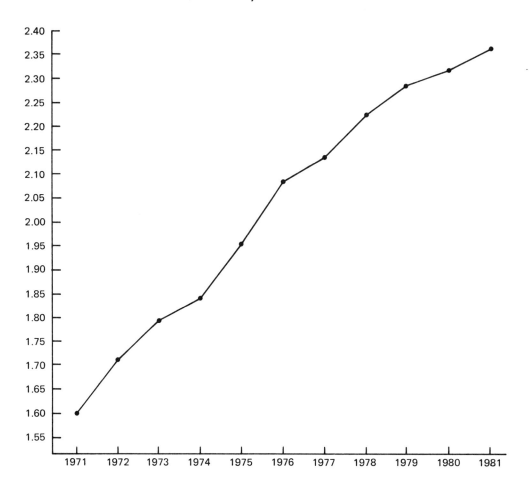

Exhibit 4. Breakdown of the Types of Construction Undertaken by Tanaka (Percentages by Sales)

	1979	1980
Offices	22.7	20.3
Stores	13.1	6.4
Hotels	4.8	7.5
Theaters	0.5	0.6
Factories	12.2	14.1
Housing	13.4	14.6
Schools	9.6	10.6
Hospitals	5.6	3.6
Government buildings	1.6	1.4
Transportation facilities	2.3	2.2
Other	14.2	18.7

Exhibit 5. Contracts Awarded Directly and Through Negotiation (Percentages)

	1979	1980
No negotiation	75.7	72.6
Negotiation	24.3	27.4

Exhibit 6. Financial and Statistical Summary of Atlas Engineering & Construction (In Millions of US$ Except Per Share Information)

	1977	1978	1979	1980	1981
Consolidated worldwide sales	742	754	1,051	1,274	1,889
Earnings after tax	24	28	38	44	45
Earnings per share	2.17	2.50	3.30	3.37	3.40
Overseas sales	298	301	337	371	378
Percent of total sales	40.2	39.9	32.1	29.1	27.2

Exhibit 7. Breakdown of the Types of Construction Undertaken by Atlas (Percentage by Sales)

	1979	1980
Dams	13.7	11.8
Bridges	23.5	26.4
Highways	4.0	5.4
Energy plants	8.7	6.2
Runways	25.6	28.7
Harbor facilities	7.4	9.3
Offshore platforms	5.7	6.1
Other	11.4	6.1

Exhibit 8. Projects in Which Atlas Was the Sole Contractor (Percentages)

1975	1976	1977	1978	1979	1980	1981
21.5	23.1	28.4	26.5	25.9	23.2	22.8

Some Points to Keep in Mind

Although a number of issues must be decided in this case, the basic concern for Tanaka revolves around its primary commitment to a single industry and hence its reputation. Something of an anomaly in Japanese business, Tanaka has bucked the "modern trend" toward diversification, concentrating instead on building and maintaining the vast majority of its business activity in a versatile but single industry. While this strategy has so far been effective, is it a policy that can withstand the multinational and diversified climate of the 1980s? Indeed, Tanaka's growth rate over the past few years, although steady, has not been great.

Related to this issue is the question of whether Tanaka stands to gain from a joint venture with Atlas. The offer does contain a partial solution to the problem of diversification within the company, since a new joint venture company would be separate from Tanaka Komuten itself and would not require Tanaka to expand its own tiny civil engineering capacity. Despite this essential difference, a new joint venture would require substantial investment capital, manpower, and other resources that would have to be diverted, at least initially, from Tanaka's main business line. In the end the decision comes down to a prediction about the future: Is the past and present direction a viable one for Tanaka in the years ahead?

CHECKLIST AND WORKSHEET

In coming to a decision about this case, did you consider the following?

Tanaka's reputation as a general contractor committed primarily to that business

The growth rates of both Tanaka and Atlas

The division in Tanaka Komuten regarding diversification

The merits/demerits of Atlas's proposal

The decrease in contracts awarded to Tanaka without negotiation

The resources required for a joint venture

What other factors should be considered?

_____

_____

_____

_____

Decision:

_____

_____

_____

_____

DISCUSSION QUESTIONS

I. Background and Dialogue
  1. Why is the strategy of specialization so important to the Tanakas?
  2. Why do some of the directors feel that Tanaka should expand its civil engineering capacity? Why does the Atlas proposal seem to benefit their position?
  3. Why does Jameson feel that a joint venture company would be to the advantage of both Tanaka and Atlas?
  4. From the Dialogue, how would you characterize Taniguchi's position? Tanaka's?

II. Exhibits and Supporting Materials
  1. Summarize the main points in Jameson's proposal (Exhibit 1). Are the advantages clearly defined? Why are the financial arrangements deliberately vague? What does the addition of two "immediate prospects" indicate?
  2. Analyze Exhibits 2 and 3. Given these figures, does it seem as if Tanaka needs a change in direction?
  3. Compare Atlas's sales with Tanaka's (Exhibit 6). Do both companies seem equally strong? What is Atlas's overseas position? Do you think this might have anything to do with its desire for an international joint venture company? Why or why not?
  4. Compare the types of construction Atlas is engaged in (Exhibit 7) in relation to the types engaged in by Tanaka (Exhibit 4). Do the companies seem to complement one another? Does this seem to support or not support a joint venture company?

EXERCISES

I. Fill in the blanks in the following paragraph with the correct word chosen from those below:

attributable   anomaly   consolidate   dilemma   diversify
drain   ironed out   precarious   prospective   tenable

Tanaka Komuten, a prosperous Japanese general contractor, began to find itself in a possibly _____ position. Something of an _____ in Japan, the company had refused to _____ its interests, preferring instead to _____ its efforts solely on building construction. Although its past success was _____ to this strategy of specialization, many wondered whether this position was still _____. When a proposal for a joint venture was received from an American firm, the _____ became even more complicated. Although many details still had to be _____, the _____ joint venture was quite attractive. If it worked out right, it looked as if Tanaka Komuten could expand into a new area without having to _____ many resources away from its main enterprise.

II. Use the information from the case to write a brief description of Tanaka Komuten. Organize your description so that it includes the following four sections:

Founding of Company/Ownership
Company Philosophy/Growth
Types of Construction
Sales (ten-year summary)

III. Summarize Tanaka Komuten's basic objections to Jameson's proposal. Use the information from the Background and Dialogue.

IV. Analyze Atlas's activities and sales (Exhibits 6 and 7). Prepare a brief report on the company using this information.

V. Expand the dialogue between Jameson, Tanaka, and Taniguchi.

Tanaka: Mr. Jameson, I really don't see that there's much advantage to our entering into a joint venture with your company.

Jameson: _____

_____

Taniguchi: Yes, we understand that it would not directly affect our status in Japan.

Jameson: _____

_____

Tanaka: Well, it's just that our reputation has been built on a policy of nondiversification.

Jameson: _____

_____

Taniguchi: I am aware that we would both remain separate as companies, but our image is at stake.

Jameson: _____

_____

VI. Study Jameson's report to Tanaka Komuten (Exhibit 1). Then write a critique of it.

VII. Perform the following guided role plays. (See Case 1 Exercises for instructions.)
   1. Jameson is discussing future projects with
      a. Tanaka Komuten
      b. the managers at Atlas
   2. Jameson is presenting his report (Exhibit 1) to the board of directors of his own company in an attempt to get their approval.
   3. Tanaka is talking with an overseas client about a new building project. The client mentions that Atlas has also approached him about doing the civil engineering work.

VIII. Debate the following. (See Case 1 Exercises for instructions.)
   1. Tanaka Komuten is behind the times. If it is going to maintain its leadership position, it must diversify.
   2. Atlas's proposal only serves Atlas, not Tanaka Komuten.

IX. Write an analysis of the case from the point of view of either Atlas or Tanaka Komuten.

6 Harding Tool Corporation

BACKGROUND

Harding Tool Corporation, an American manufacturer of large and small machine tools and parts, gears, valves, and bearings, was a major supplier to industries and companies worldwide. Because of the rise of the U.S. dollar on foreign exchange markets and serious financial crises in many of the countries in which Harding did business, sales, particularly to Latin America, began to decline.

A major market for Harding's products had until recently been Brazil. For instance, in 1980 sales to that country's industries were $640,000; but by 1983 sales had declined to just $183,000. This serious problem seemed to have little solution because of Brazil's chronic credit problems and lack of foreign exchange. In the fall of 1984, however, a unique proposition was received at Harding's head office near Cleveland, Ohio, from a Brazilian commodities broker, Companhia Internacional de Comércio, S.A. (CIC). CIC's offer was essentially this: In exchange for US$400,000 in assorted gears, Harding would receive the equivalent in Brazilian shoes, which it could sell in the American market.

Harding's first reaction was to reject the deal; indeed, the overseas sales manager, Lloyd Wilcox, found the arrangement almost laughable. On further consideration, however, he began to think more seriously about the proposition. Four hundred thousand dollars was a significant amount of money. But what would a machine tool manufacturer do with shoes?

DIALOGUE: CONSIDERING A COUNTERTRADE PROPOSAL

CAST: Lloyd Wilcox, Overseas Sales Manager, Harding Tool Corp.

José Cabral, President, Companhia Internacional de Comércio

Mr. Wilcox is talking on the telephone to Mr. Cabral.

Wilcox: I must confess, Mr. Cabral, that at first your offer seemed completely out of the question, but after talking with my associates, we decided we might as well investigate it.

Cabral: I'm sure it must have seemed unusual to you at first, but it's one way Brazil has managed to cope with its foreign exchange problems.

Wilcox: Obviously, we're happy to sell you $400,000 worth of gears. But what in the world are we to do with shoes? We have absolutely no use for shoes and know nothing about selling them.

Cabral: There are a couple of actions you can take. You can arrange to transfer title to a middleman, say an importer there in the U.S., or you can do as some companies have done—Sears, G.M. or Citicorp, for instance—and set up a trading subsidiary of your own.

Wilcox: I can't see us setting up a trading company. What I can see is my boss laughing me out of the office for even suggesting it.

Cabral: That's usually the first reaction. But a company such as yours that deals extensively in the Third World might want to consider it.

Wilcox: Well, that's another matter. What about this deal? How would it work?

Cabral: It's really fairly simple. You send us $400,000 in parts—we send you the title for $400,000 in shoes. When you sell the shoes, we'll deliver them wherever you want. That way you don't have to house them.

Wilcox: Hmm. But suppose we can't sell the shoes?

Cabral: That shouldn't be a problem. They're excellent shoes, and the price is extremely low.

Wilcox: But I don't know anything about shoes! I don't know what a good shoe is or what a good price is.

Cabral: That's where the specialist comes in. If you hand the deal over to a commodities specialist, he should be able to evaluate the product and sell it.

Wilcox: I don't know. The whole business sounds very risky.

Cabral: It's not risky. You can even make an extra profit on it.

Wilcox: How?

Cabral: Take a small commission on the sale of the shoes, say 2–3 percent.

Wilcox: Well, Mr. Cabral, I obviously can't make a decision now. Let me talk to some commodity specialists and to my associates. Maybe if they feel we can move the shoes, we might consider it. I think, I should say, I know, that Harding is going to be reluctant to ship $400,000 worth of gears without first having some assurance we will actually get paid. Do this for me—send me the specs on the shoes—even some samples. Also, a breakdown on what gears you want to purchase. Then, we can talk some more.

Cabral: Okay, I'll get the shoes off to you right away and also a tentative order for your gears. Thanks for considering this proposal. I feel sure we can work something out.

EXHIBITS AND SUPPORTING MATERIALS

Exhibit I. Information from Cabral Regarding Shoes

Companhia Internacional de Comércio, S.A.
Rua do Acre 87
20081 Rio de Janeiro, R.J., Brasil
Tel.: (021)232-4624
Telex: 6782986

OFFER TO SELL

General Description: 13,200 men's shoes; 31,670 women's shoes

Total Price: US$400,000 C.I.F.

Styles:

Men's

Oxfords—leather uppers and soles; brown, black, gray, burgundy

Loafers—leather uppers and soles; brown, black, burgundy, tan

---

Casual Lace-ups—leather uppers, crepe soles, foam insole;
        natural dark brown

Women's

Pumps—leather uppers and soles; black, brown, navy, red,
        burgundy, gray

Pumps—leather uppers, man-made material soles; black, brown,
        navy, burgundy, taupe

Flats—leather uppers, crepe soles; red, black, blue, white,
        gray, burgundy

Sandals—leather uppers and soles; natural light brown, natural
        dark brown, black, tan, navy

C.I.F. Prices (US$):

Men's

Oxfords, 4,500 @ 13.50
Loafers, 6,200 @ 12.00
Casuals, 2,500 @ 9.00

Women's

Pumps (all leather), 8,000 @ 10.00
Pumps (man-made soles), 12,000 @ 8.00
Flats, 4,000 @ 7.00
Sandals, 7,670 @ 5.00

U.S. Sizes

Men's

7, 7½, 8, 8½, 9, 9½, 10, 10½, 11, 11½, 12, 12½
Widths: B, C, D, some E

Women's

5, 5½, 6, 6½, 7, 7½, 8, 8½, 9, 9½, 10
Widths: some A, B, C

Please see accompanying samples and literature.

Exhibit 2. Harding's Gross Sales to Latin America, 1976–1983 (In Thousands of US$)

	1976	1977	1978	1979	1980	1981	1982	1983
Argentina	—	—	126	114	83	197	112	133
Brazil	264	327	431	524	640	342	206	183
Colombia	324	531	589	320	512	434	486	472
Venezuela	434	576	484	372	464	207	181	192
Mexico	312	236	174	189	76	62	41	77
Chile	—	—	—	—	—	122	221	204
Other	120	170	330	410	474	314	306	284
Total	1,454	1,840	2,134	1,929	2,249	1,678	1,553	1,545
Percentage of total gross sales	7.8	6.5	8.9	10.7	10.2	9.8	8.2	6.1

Exhibit 3. Letter from Julia Peters, Commodities Broker, to Lloyd Wilcox

Overseas Development Corporation
International Commodities Brokers
64 W. 56th St.
New York, NY 10019
(212)489-7019

September 21, 1984

Mr. Lloyd Wilcox
Overseas Sales Manager
Harding Tool Corporation
16263 South Miles
Warrensville Heights, Ohio 44128

Dear Mr. Wilcox:

Thank you for your phone call on Wednesday. Today the information and samples of Brazilian shoes arrived at the office by express mail. As we discussed in our conversation, we do specialize in handling countertrade consignments. After examining the offer to sell and the samples, we feel we could indeed place these shoes. Additional information from the seller, however, is necessary. Specifically, we need to know the exact quantities of shoes in various sizes, widths, and colors. We can either obtain this information directly from the seller, or you can contact your client. If the offer meets the general requirements of our potential buyers, we would be delighted to proceed with the arrangement.

Please note that we charge a 2 percent commission for placing your goods.

Let us know as soon as possible how you wish to proceed with obtaining the additional information. Hoping to do business with you soon.

Sincerely yours,

Julia Peters

Julia Peters
President

Exhibit 4. Minutes from Meeting of Harding Executives to Discuss the Brazilian Offer

Minutes of Meeting, September 26, 1984

Present: F. Garret, L. Wilcox, M. Ross, C. Carmichael, P. Lamoreux, R. Kaplan (Recording Secretary)

The meeting began at 9:45 A.M. in the conference room.

Mr. Wilcox presented the details of the offer from Companhia Internacional de Comércio and the letter from J. Peters, a commodities broker in New York (see attached photocopies).

Mr. Garret questioned whether Harding was so desperate that it needed to get into the shoe business.

Mr. Wilcox answered by saying that while Harding was not ''desperate,'' countertrade was becoming more common, particularly with countries experiencing foreign exchange problems. Ms. Carmichael added that barter or countertrade was used by many large companies in order to maintain clients in economically troubled regions and that Harding should think about doing the same.

Mr. Ross suggested that if the deal were accepted, Harding should add 5—10 percent on to the cost of the gears to cover additional costs (commissions) incurred by the arrangement.

Ms. Carmichael said that this was customary and feasible. She added that Harding was in a ''seller's market'' as far as Brazil was concerned.

Ms. Lamoreux expressed her concern that no goods should be shipped until Harding was sure they could actually sell the shoes. Mr. Wilcox agreed. Mr. Garret felt strongly that the title to the shoes should be received before ''even one gear'' was shipped. Mr. Ross, Ms. Carmichael, and Mr. Wilcox agreed.

Mr. Garret moved that the meeting be adjourned. Mr. Wilcox argued that no decision had been made. Mr. Garret said that he thought it had been decided to investigate the matter further, bearing in mind the ideas discussed in the meeting. All agreed that this was correct. Mr. Garret asked to be informed of the progress. He said he would make a decision on cost increases to cover commissions depending on Mr. Wilcox's investigation.

The meeting was adjourned at 10:41 A.M.

Respectfully submitted,

Rosemary Kaplan

Rosemary Kaplan
Recording Secretary

Some Points to Keep in Mind

Although relatively unknown a few years ago, countertrade—the exchanging of goods for goods—is becoming more common in international business dealings. Originally confined primarily to trading between Eastern and Western Europe, countertrade is now a worldwide phenomenon. The exchange of goods is generally concentrated between Western manufacturing countries and developing countries. Usually the Western company sends highly specialized items (cars, cameras, computers) to a developing country; a company in the developing country (or a middleman representing that country) sends less specialized goods (shoes, bicycles, tuna) to the Western nation.

In this case, the exchange is precision gears for shoes. Harding must decide whether it is worthwhile to accept the shoes (a commodity for which it has no use) in order to increase sales in Brazil. There are certain risks involved on both sides. Unless the Brazilian trading firm has a customer already lined up for the gears, it may find itself with merchandise it cannot sell; on the other hand, Harding must find a way to "unload" the shoes in order to ensure a return on its sale.

Recently a number of firms specializing in countertrade have been established. Although a few major corporations have set up subsidiary companies to market goods received through countertrade, most companies find they need to use a specialist. These specialist firms, sometimes called transit houses, are often offshoots of banks or commodity houses. Some have been highly successful, with annual profits in the millions of dollars; others have quickly gone bankrupt. Many critics argue that countertrade is bad for business and commerce. But with the rise of the dollar on foreign exchange markets and increasingly tight credit in many developing countries, it is obvious that countertrade is one method to maintain international trade.

CHECKLIST AND WORKSHEET

In coming to a decision about this case, did you consider the following?

Harding's declining sales to Latin America

The financial risk of countertrade

The precedent being established if Harding should decide to take the shoes in exchange for gears

The relative importance of Brazil as a market

The possible financial gain versus the complications and extra work involved for Harding

What other factors should be considered?

_____

_____

_____

_____

Decision:

_____

_____

_____

_____

DISCUSSION QUESTIONS

I. Background and Dialogue
1. Why have Harding's overseas sales, particularly to Latin America, drastically declined?
2. Why did Wilcox initially find the Brazilian offer almost laughable?
3. How does Cabral try to convince Wilcox that a barter arrangement makes good sense?
4. By the end of the Dialogue, how has Wilcox's position changed regarding the barter arrangement? Why?

II. Exhibits and Supporting Materials
1. Does the information in Exhibit 1 seem complete? If not, what specific type of information is missing?
2. How does Exhibit 2 seem to confirm Cabral's assessment in the Dialogue that a company dealing a lot with the Third World ought to consider countertrade?
3. Does Exhibit 3 seem to be a positive response to Wilcox's inquiry? If so, why? If not, why not?
4. Given Mr. Garret's statements as reported in the minutes of the meeting (Exhibit 4), what would you say his position is in the company? How would you characterize his attitude? Ms. Carmichael's?

EXERCISES

I. Look at the following phrase from the Dialogue:

> . . . after talking with my *associates*, we decided we might as well investigate it.

In this sentence, *associates* is used as a noun to mean colleagues. Other forms of *associate* include its verb form, *to associate;* its adjective forms, *associate, associated,* and *associative;* and its adverb form, *associatively.* Although all of these words are related, they are all used in sentences in different ways; in some cases the meaning is also different. In the following exercise, write new sentences using the designated forms. All of the sentences are drawn from the case.

1. After talking with my *associates,* we decided we might as well investigate it.

   associated (adj) _____

   _____

   associate (v) _____

   _____

2. After talking with my associates, we decided we might as well *investigate* it.

   investigator (n) _____

   _____

   investigation (n) _____

   _____

   investigative (adj) _____

   _____

3. We have *absolutely* no use for shoes and know nothing about selling them.

   absolute (adj) _____

   _____

   absoluteness (n) _____

   _____

4. Harding's first *reaction* was to reject the deal.

react (v) _____

_____

reactive (adj) _____

_____

5. On further *consideration*, however, he began to think more seriously about the *proposition*.

consider (v) _____

_____

considerable (adj) _____

_____

considerably (adv) _____

_____

propose (v) _____

_____

proposed (adj) _____

_____

6. He should be able to *evaluate* the product and sell it.

evaluator (n) _____

_____

evaluative (adj) _____

_____

evaluation (n) _____

_____

7. We do specialize in handling *consignments*.

consign (v) _____

_____

consignee (n) _____

_____

consignor (n) _____

_____

8. There are certain risks *involved* on both sides.

risk (v) _____

_____

risky (adj) _____

_____

II. Summarize the Background using the clues provided to you below.

Harding Tool Corporation was an American manufacturer of large

and small machine tools and parts, gears, valves, and bearings. In

the fall of 1984, Harding received _____

_____.

Companhia Internacional de Comércio offered to exchange _____

_____

_____.

Lloyd Wilcox, _____

_____.

After thinking it over, though, _____

_____.

At the same time, he wondered _____

_____.

III. Expand the dialogue between Cabral and Wilcox.

Wilcox: Suppose we do work out a deal. As you probably realize, I can't send you any gears until I get some shoes.

Cabral: _____

_____

Wilcox: No, I'm afraid we'll need more than just an official notice that the shoes have been sent. Also, we'll need to inspect them to make sure they are exactly what was specified.

Cabral: _____

_____

Wilcox: It isn't that we don't trust you. It's just that we have to make sure. We're new at this business, you know.

Cabral: _____

_____

Wilcox: Well, I hope so. I'll get back to you as soon as my boss makes a decision.

Cabral: _____

_____

IV. In the Background you read these sentences:

> A major market for Harding's products had until recently been Brazil. For instance, in 1980 sales to that country's industries were $640,000; but by 1983 sales had declined to just $183,000.

The first sentence above is an assertion. It states a fact. The second sentence provides proof of the assertion through the use of examples. Using numerical data from Exhibit 2, write some more assertions and proofs to support your statements.

Example: Harding's sales to Argentina in 1981 were more than double what they were in 1980. In 1980 they were just $83,000; in 1981 they were $197,000.

1. _____

_____

_____

2. _____

_____

_____

3. _____

_____

_____

4. _____

_____

_____

5. _____

_____

_____

V. In Exhibit 3, Wilcox receives a letter from Julia Peters, the president of a commodities firm. Peters asks Wilcox to provide some further information on the shoes. Write one of the following letters:
   a. Wilcox to Cabral requesting further details about the shoes.
   b. Cabral to Wilcox giving the information.
   c. Wilcox to Peters giving the information received from Cabral.

VI. Exhibit 4 contains the minutes from a meeting. From the following notes, write your own minutes:

10/4/84

Attending: F. Garret, L. Wilcox, C. Carmichael, (Your Name, recording
      secretary).

Meeting began/2:30 P.M./conference room.

LW presented details/letter Cabral, 9/31/84. Said telephone

response/Peters/New York/positive.

FG questioned shipping dates. Wanted written confirmation/

acceptance/Peters.

LW said O.K. Could get. If O.K./CIF NY/late Nov., Dec.

CC asked/Harding's shipping/Brazil

LW said after Cabral's shipment delivered/inspected.

FG said O.K.

All agreed.

Adjourned 2:50 P.M.

VII. Perform the following guided role plays. (See Case 1 Exercises for instructions.)
   1. Wilcox is talking on the phone to Cabral to arrange the final aspects of the deal. He tells him that Harding will have to charge 5 percent more for the gears to cover the broker's commission.
   2. Peters is talking to a shoe buyer about selling the Brazilian shoes.
   3. Wilcox is discussing the deal with his colleagues and Garret.

VIII. Debate the following issues. (See Case 1 Exercises for instructions.)
1. Barter is the best way for Third World countries to obtain goods without having to use foreign exchange.
2. Barter only benefits Third World countries, not the West.

IX. Write an analysis of the case from the point of view of either Wilcox, Cabral, or Peters.

7 Comtec Corporation

BACKGROUND

In January 1984, Comtec Corporation, a small manufacturer of industrial microcomputers and application-specific software in Cambridge, Massachusetts, was having a difficult time competing in both the domestic and international markets. Sales of its primary product, the Comtec 100 Microcomputer, were slow, and the company's profit was practically nonexistent. In short, Comtec was facing a serious financial crisis.

In an attempt to save the company, the president, Dr. Daniel Needham, hired an outside consultant, Ms. Roberta Malcolm, a seasoned professional with years of high-tech marketing experience. After studying the situation for a couple of weeks, Ms. Malcolm made three recommendations. The first called for closing down the European sales office in Amsterdam and concentrating, for the present at least, on the U.S. market. The second recommendation was for Comtec to shift from a hardware to software emphasis. Specifically, Ms. Malcolm advised the company to begin producing IBM-compatible software for general-purpose laboratory/technical uses. Her third recommendation called for the company to shift its advertising and sales promotion from heavy reliance on journal advertising and press releases to direct mail advertising and trade show exhibits.

All three conclusions, though not explicitly critical of the vice-president for sales and marketing, Mr. Harry Otto, were implicitly so since Mr. Otto had been instrumental in implementing the present marketing strategy. It was now up to the company to decide whether to risk its remaining capital on an entirely new direction or stay with the present course, namely, continuing Mr. Otto's strategy of industry-specific hardware/software production.

DIALOGUE: A NEW MARKETING STRATEGY?

CAST: Dr. Daniel Needham, President, Comtec Corporation

Mr. Harry Otto, Vice-President, Comtec Corporation

Ms. Roberta Malcolm, Computer Consultant

The three are discussing Ms. Malcolm's report in Dr. Needham's office at Comtec.

Malcolm: Let me just say at the beginning that I realize my recommendations may seem very bold, but given the present financial situation at Comtec I think bold measures are needed.

Otto: Right on both counts. The question is, are these the right measures? My feeling is simply that we haven't been aggressive enough in our marketing. Also, the new targeted fields—materials-testing automation and chromatography automation—are not quick sells; it takes some time to build up orders. We launched our new campaign in the early fall; it's just January now. I think you're premature in your assessment that this is not the right market.

Needham: Harry's right to some extent. But the truth is the orders just aren't coming in fast enough. We can't play a long-term waiting game. We don't have the capital to last.

Otto: All right. Orders aren't coming in in the necessary quantity, but we're getting more and more inquiries, and with proper action we should be able to turn them into orders.

Malcolm: Mr. Otto, I understand your position, but I don't feel that you've received enough inquiries to warrant optimism.

Otto: I'm not that optimistic at all about it, but I feel we have to give this market, this product, some chance.

Needham: Harry, what are you basing your sales projections on?

Otto: First, our sales manager in Amsterdam, Max Mendel, is right now working on an order for ten Comtecs, plus software. That amounts to $200,000.

Malcolm: But an order isn't an order until you get a P.O.* number.

Otto: Right. But Max feels confident he'll get it.

Needham: That brings up the whole matter of the European sales office.

Malcolm: Yes, it does. And I can't see that it's worth keeping. It doesn't even pay for itself.

*purchase order

Needham: Well, I don't think that's true. But it barely pays for itself.

Otto: Ms. Malcolm's correct, Dan. It hasn't paid for itself in four months. I still don't feel that means we should shut it down. The potential is there. Max is a good sales rep, and things are beginning to turn.

Malcolm: Gentlemen, let me make a couple of things clear. I was hired by you to do a study and make some recommendations. I did that. It's your choice whether to accept the recommendations or not. I happen to think my recommendations are sound, but it's up to you to decide. The reasons I think they are sound are detailed in the report, but let me just reiterate a few facts here. First, in three months of active effort you have only six orders. Second, the competition, particularly in chromatography, is keen. Third, the European sales office is costing more than it's producing. Fourth, your microcomputer is too expensive, given the fact that an IBM PC costs one-fourth as much as the Comtec and is an industry standard. Granted, it may not do as much, but it is basically all most researchers need, given the right software. If you convert your software so that it will run on the IBM PC, you'll be in a position to do just that. And if you are more horizontal than vertical in your approach to the market, you'll have a larger target. Fifth, your advertising and sales promotion measures are not getting to the right people. Buy some lists and then do a direct mail shot. Go to every trade show you can and demonstrate your product. The audience you're trying to reach doesn't take journal advertising seriously. They want more information than they can get in an ad. Direct mail can give that to them; a demo can do even more.

EXHIBITS AND SUPPORTING MATERIALS

Exhibit 1. Ad for the Comtec 100 Microcomputers

Automate Your Lab NOW

When is laboratory automation more than just laboratory automation? When you automate with a Comtec 100—the most powerful R & D micro on the market. The Comtec 100 features multitasking, multiprocessing, ultra-high-speed analog input, and a

real-time operating system. These features make the Comtec 100
capable of being a central computer for all your automation needs.
Special application-specific programs for Materials Testing and
Chromatography, as well as general-purpose R & D software, make
Comtec a leader in laboratory automation.

Call, Write, or Circle Inquiry No. for Action

Comtec Corporation
333 Roadway
Cambridge, MA
1-800-262-8400

Circle Reader Service Card No. 363

Exhibit 2. Sales of the Comtec 100, Third and Fourth Quarter, 1983 (in US$)

	July	Aug.	Sept.	Oct.	Nov.	Dec.	Total
Domestic	38,900	48,600	61,642	54,282	42,623	43,624	289,671
International	31,090	21,438	37,583	21,438	21,438	—	132,987
							422,658

Exhibit 3. Comtec's Balance Sheet as of December 1983 (Actual US$)

ASSETS	
Cash	44,190
Accounts receivable:	
trade	209,540
other	41,800
Inventories:	
raw materials	98,070
packaging	24,504
work in progress	3,230
finished goods	107,440
Prepaid expenses	10,756
TOTAL CURRENT ASSETS	539,530

Fixed assets	12,462
less depreciation	(4,790)
Net fixed assets	7,672
Other noncurrent	190
TOTAL ASSETS	547,392
LIABILITIES	
Notes payable	54,182
Accounts payable:	
trade	269,904
current intercompany	82,591
accrued expenses	23,693
accrued taxes	97,330
TOTAL CURRENT LIABILITIES	527,700
Reserves	1,561
Share capital (privately held)	18,131
TOTAL LIABILITIES	547,392

Exhibit 4. Memo from H. Otto to D. Needham

Interoffice Memorandum

To: D. Needham
Fm: H.A.O.
Re: Direct Mail
Date: Jan. 23, 1984

I contacted the people at Industrial Collaborative today in an effort
to purchase direct mail lists. They claim to have very vertical lists
of primary purchasers both in the U.S. and abroad for materials-
testing automation and chromatography automation. They will sell one
list for $1,200 or two for $2,100 (over 1,000 names in each). The lists
include names and titles. I strongly suggest we purchase the lists, as
recommended by Ms. Malcolm, and create a direct mail piece to accompany

existing product literature. David, at International Communications, says he can have design and copy in a matter of days for a four-page brochure describing our automation packages. He will check back later today to confirm. Let's talk this afternoon.

Exhibit 5. Letter from Manchester Metals, Ltd., to Comtec's Amsterdam Office

MANCHESTER METALS, LTD.
4, Surrey Rd.
Manchester, England

27 January, 1984

Mr Max Mendel
Comtec Corporation
Brouwersgracht 77
Amsterdam, Netherlands

Dear Mr Mendel:

I enjoyed talking with you last week when you were in Manchester and am pleased to report that I was quite impressed with the Comtec 100 Microcomputer. I have recommended to the purchasing section that one Comtec 100 be purchased as soon as possible. The order should be sent to you within ten days. As I informed you last week, our long-term needs could conceivably call for additional purchases of eight to twelve Comtecs. This initial purchase, therefore, should be viewed as a trial. I have few doubts, however, that the Comtec 100 will perform to our complete satisfaction.

Looking forward to doing more business with you.

Most sincerely yours,

Susan T. West

Susan T. West, Ph.D.
Director, Mechanical Testing

Some Points to Keep in Mind

Business strategies, by their very nature, are continually subject to change. Regardless of a company's past performance, innovative ideas are absolutely essential if the company wishes to increase or even maintain its market share. Since business is not a science, however, it is impossible to determine exactly how long a particular strategy should be employed before it is changed. Premature shifts in marketing strategy often have negative results. At the same time, in order to minimize losses, it is important to recognize when a strategy is not successful so that it may be altered.

In this case, the dilemma is precisely that described above. Comtec's strategy initially was to produce microcomputers for general industrial use. When that was not successful, Comtec targeted two specific areas: materials-testing automation and chromatography automation. Now, that strategy too seems to be failing. Is it, however, the case, as Mr. Otto believes, that simply more time is needed to penetrate these special targets, both domestically and overseas, or is a new direction needed? Finally, is the radical change proposed by Ms. Malcolm the right direction if Comtec should decide to change its strategy?

CHECKLIST AND WORKSHEET

In coming to a decision about this case, did you consider the following?

Malcolm's recommendations

Otto's original marketing strategy

The importance of the European office

The poor financial situation of Comtec

Otto's revised strategy

The risks involved in radically changing the nature of the corporation

What other factors should be considered?

_____

_____

_____

Decision:

DISCUSSION QUESTIONS

   I. Background and Dialogue
1. What does Comtec Corporation do? What is its major product? For what market does it manufacture?
2. What are Malcolm's three major recommendations?
3. How would you characterize Otto's position regarding the new marketing strategy? Needham's?
4. At the end of the Dialogue Malcolm has a very long speech in which she lays out her recommendations. What is the overall effect of that speech? Is her tone authoritative or weak? Are her points clearly made? Do the recommendations seem to help support the issues raised earlier in the Dialogue?

  II. Exhibits and Supporting Materials
1. Analyze the ad in Exhibit 1. Is it easily understandable or too technical? Does it seem appropriate for the audience it is trying to reach? If yes, how? If not, how could it be improved?
2. Exhibits 2 and 3 show Comtec's financial situation. Judging from these figures, is Comtec in serious trouble? Support your answer with specific references to the exhibits.
3. Does Exhibit 3 suggest that Otto is adopting Malcolm's suggestions? Why or why not?
4. Evaluate West's letter (Exhibit 4). Does it seem encouraging? In your opinion, what do the following sentences really indicate?

> . . . our long-term needs could conceivably call for additional purchases of eight to twelve Comtecs. This initial purchase, therefore, should be viewed as a trial.

EXERCISES

I. Look at this sentence from the Background:

> All three conclusions, though not *explicitly* critical of the vice-president for sales and marketing, Mr. Harry Otto, were *implicitly* so.

Explicitly and *implicitly* both begin with prefixes. The prefix *ex* means out, from, beyond, away from, or without. The prefix *im* means in, into, within, on, not, no, or without. *Im* is used only before the letters *m, p,* or *b;* otherwise, the more common prefix *in,* which means the same thing, is used. In the above sentence the *ex* in *explicitly* has the meaning of out; a synonym of *explicitly* is *outwardly*. *Implicitly* means exactly the opposite, *im* having the meaning of in as in *inwardly*.

In the following exercise, match the word on the left with its definition on the right. Try to use the prefixes to help you define them. All the words are taken from the case, and all have *ex, im, in,* or *inter* prefixes.

a. exactly	1. costs
b. examine	2. between divisions of a company
c. existent	3. concerned
d. expensive	4. strictly
e. expenses	5. serving as a means to do something
f. extent	6. new; original
g. implement	7. inspect carefully
h. important	8. concerned with
i. impossible	9. to put into practice
j. increase	10. to have being
k. initially	11. between or among nations
l. innovative	12. of much significance
m. instrumental	13. costly
n. intercompany	14. degree to which a thing extends
o. international	15. unable to be done
p. involved	16. to make greater

II. In the Background a number of problems with Comtec are mentioned, either directly or indirectly by way of proposed changes. Make a list of these problems. Then, for each, write a one-sentence statement describing it.

III. Prepare an outline (formal or informal) for Ms. Malcolm's report to Comtec. Your outline should include detailed sections analyzing both the present situation and giving specific recommendations for the future. Use the information from the Background and the Dialogue to help you.

IV. Write a brief summary of the balance sheet in Exhibit 3. Your analysis should include a comparison between assets and liabilities. Note that while the total assets and total liabilities are exactly the same (and must be if a balance sheet is to "balance"), there are a number of points to compare: total current assets versus total current liabilities, accounts receivable versus accounts payable, cash versus notes payable, etc. From your comparison, how would you rate the financial situation of the company?

V. Create a graph for Exhibit 2, showing the domestic and international sales trends for the third and fourth quarters of 1983.

VI. Create a dialogue between Needham and Otto regarding Exhibit 4.

Needham: Harry, it seems as if you're missing the basic points of Ms. Malcolm's recommendations.

Otto: _____

Needham: I say that because her report explicitly states that we should abandon these markets and change our direction.

Otto: _____

Needham: I know you believe we should give it more time, but we don't have more time.

Otto: _____

Needham: Well, maybe I am making a mistake, but we've got to try to get a product that actually sells.

Otto: _____

VII. Perform the following guided role plays. (See Case 1 Exercises for instructions.)
1. Otto is demonstrating the Comtec 100 to a customer.
2. Mendel is trying to persuade Needham not to close the European office.
3. Mendel is talking to Susan West at Manchester Metals as a follow-up to West's letter and as a way of trying to get more orders for Comtec.
4. Otto, Needham, and an advertising executive are meeting to discuss the new product strategy.

VIII. Debate one of the following topics. (See Case 1 Exercises for instructions.)
1. Needham should listen to Otto, not Malcolm.
2. Otto is not willing to accept new ideas.
3. A successful business must continually seek new and dynamic solutions and strategies.

IX. Write an analysis of the case from the point of view of either Otto or Needham.

8 Hanover Public Systems

BACKGROUND

Hanover Public Systems (HPS), an American manufacturer of industrial electrical equipment, including elevators, lighting systems, heating and cooling equipment, and industrial fans, began to establish foreign manufacturing subsidiaries in the early 1960s. By 1982 the company had eight wholly-owned subsidiaries abroad in addition to its four large domestic plants. The financial performance of the foreign subsidiaries was good, with the exception of the Taiwan facility, which had been losing money at a precipitous rate since 1980.

At midyear 1982 the Taipei office reported further substantial losses despite an infusion of $3 million from the parent company earlier in the year. After considerable study and deliberation, the president of the Taiwan plant, Yang Hsiao-shih, was fired. He was replaced by James Fukuda, a second-generation Japanese-American who had formerly been vice-president of operations at the Oakland, California, plant. At 38, Fukuda was the youngest person ever to become a Hanover president. Regarded by the head HPS office in New York as a brilliant manager, Fukuda had initiated policies during his three-year tenure in Oakland, including a much-needed managerial reorganization, that had resulted in phenomenal growth. In the opinion of the head office, he was clearly the best person to take over the ailing subsidiary.

Upon being named subsidiary president, and even before arriving in Taipei, Fukuda began to make changes. His first action was to dispose of a part of the assets and inventory in order to offset liabilities, a course that had been rejected by his predecessor, Mr. Yang. His second action, after just one week in Taiwan, was to shut down the manufacturing of heating and cooling equipment, a decision completely opposed by the all-Taiwanese staff at HPS—Taiwan. This action, resulting in the layoff of eighteen workers and the reassignment of twelve more, drew considerable heat from the workers. Fukuda's third action, after just one month on the job, was to introduce a radically new management system.

This last decision finally outraged the executives to a point where both the vice-president for operations and the plant superintendent resigned. The middle- and upper-level managers sent a letter to the president of HPS, Howard Wolff, expressing their dismay with Fukuda and seriously questioning his policies. Wolff, who had conceived and engineered the establishment of HPS—Taiwan and who had worked closely with a number of the letter's signatories, began himself to wonder whether Fukuda was maybe moving just a little too fast.

DIALOGUE: A POLICY DISCUSSION

CAST: Howard Wolff, President, HPS

James Fukuda, President, HPS—Taiwan

Mr. Fukuda has just been informed by his secretary that Mr. Wolff is on the line from New York.

Fukuda: Howard?
Wolff: Jim, how are you?
Fukuda: Good thanks. What's up?
Wolff: Well, I'm calling for a couple of reasons. I'll get the small matter out of the way first. I need a complete inventory update a.s.a.p.
Fukuda: Okay. Next.
Wolff: Jim, I trust you got a copy of the letter sent to me by Lo and thirteen others.
Fukuda: Yeah, I saw it.
Wolff: It's too bad we had to lose Hu and Lee. They were good people.
Fukuda: I was surprised myself at their resignations. But I guess they felt they had to do it to save face.
Wolff: You couldn't persuade them otherwise?
Fukuda: They didn't give me much of a chance. They obviously had their minds made up.
Wolff: I see. Well, how are things there now?
Fukuda: To be honest, Howard, it's tough going. In fact, I've got some-

thing of a rebellion on my hands at the moment. It'll pass soon, though. Once the managers realize that the changes I want to make are for their own good, I think we'll see some real changes in attitude.

Wolff: That may be true, but they're upset now, and I'm not sure we can afford that. Morale hasn't been so hot for some time there, and it seems we've gone from bad to worse. And that's counterproductive to anything we might want to do in terms of recovery.

Fukuda: But, Howard, that's to be expected. Give it some time. The point is we can't wait for people to be happy with every decision to initiate some new measures here. As you know, Yang pleased everybody in this company for years while driving it to the point of bankruptcy. I'm not interested in alienating the people that I have to work with, but at the same time I'm not trying to win any popularity awards either. Certain measures had to be taken and taken immediately. I took them. And already we have current assets in excess of current liabilities.

Wolff: Jim, I know, and I'm not questioning your fiscal policies. I am wondering, though, if maybe you could hold off a bit on the reorganization. My personal feeling is that with all the other changes going on this is not the best thing to take on right now. When you reorganized in Oakland, it worked fine because the operation itself was sound and because you were not perceived by middle-management as an outsider. But you're in Taiwan, Jim, not Oakland. And that matters.

Fukuda: I know I'm in Taiwan, and I know that I'm resented because I'm not Taiwanese. At the same time, I'm doing what I feel I have to do to save this subsidiary. And a reshuffle is one of those measures.

Wolff: But, Jim, you're not running Taiwan by yourself. You're making the key decisions, sure, and that's what we expect you to do, but you've got to have cooperation if those decisions are truly to be implemented.

Fukuda: I'm well aware of that. I admit I may have moved a little too fast with reorganization. But one of the main problems here *is* the organization. It's got to be dealt with. They'll come around. Right now, everybody's on edge—threatened, worried. Also because I'm Japanese-American it's worse.

Wolff: What does that have to do with it?

Fukuda: The Chinese don't like the Japanese. History, you know.

Wolff: Oh, come on.

Fukuda: I'm serious.

Wolff: Well, nobody there is bringing that up.

Fukuda: Not to you, maybe, but I can feel it. Anyway, it doesn't matter. What matters is that we're making progress. And you'll see, as we start to make a profit again, the attitudes will change.

Wolff: I just hope that you're right and that the attitudes won't get in the way of making a profit. Do make an effort to communicate, though. It's vital. Talk it out with them. Get their advice. They know and care a lot about the business.

EXHIBITS AND SUPPORTING MATERIALS

Exhibit 1. Letter from Lo to Wolff

HPS—Taiwan   *A Subsidiary of Hanover Public Systems, Inc.*

44 Pei-An Rd.   Telephone: (923)6634
Taipei, Republic of China   Telex: 32334J

Mr. Howard Wolff
President
Hanover Public Systems
244 Park Ave.
New York, N.Y. 10020

Dear Mr. Wolff:

We, the middle- and upper-level managers at HPS—Taiwan, are writing to you as a last resort. As you are well aware, the financial situation at our company has necessitated a number of changes designed to increase our profitability. Among the measures instituted by President Fukuda are partial liquidation, cessation of manufacturing heating and cooling systems, and managerial reorganization. While we understand the need for sweeping changes for cost-effective reasons, we take issue with two of Mr. Fukuda's actions—his decision to halt production of heating and cooling systems and his reorganization plan.

Although none of us would argue that heating and cooling systems have been profitable during the last two years, Mr. Fukuda's action does not take into consideration a number of factors. One, the decline in sales has been due chiefly to artificially low prices set by our competition (mainly Japanese manufacturers) in an attempt to drive us out of the market. It is clear that their profit margin (if any) is small and

---

therefore cannot continue nor be indicative of the fair market value of
the product. If we were to lower our prices substantially, we too could
compete in this current price war. Two, Mr. Fukuda is ignoring the
hardship placed on laid-off and reassigned workers. Within the
factory, these layoffs have resulted in depressed morale among the
workers on other assembly lines. Surely, halting production of these
systems is not the only viable solution available to him.

The other matter that concerns us is Mr. Fukuda's American-style (or
Japanese-style) reorganization plan. In our collective opinion, it is
extremely unwise. There are three main problems with it. First, it
consolidates sales in one division. Although this may be more
immediately cost effective, in the long run it may seriously affect the
reputation and sales of Hanover Taiwan, since sales of our equipment
are dependent upon our sales force having a specialized knowledge of
the product they are selling. Under Mr. Fukuda's plan, salesmen will
sell all Hanover products, even those that they may not be familiar
with, a situation that could backfire if the product sold is not
appropriate to the client's needs.

Second, Mr. Fukuda has so far not designated who will be in charge of
what division after the reorganization. He claims he ''wants to see us
in action'' before he makes a decision. This creates unfair anxiety
among all of us, since we do not know whether we are to be promoted,
demoted, or even fired.

Third, Mr. Fukuda has created this plan without consulting us and
without having any knowledge of the intricacies of doing business in
the Republic of China. Since we are all native Chinese with years of
accumulated business experience, we deeply resent his manner of
dealing. This lack of regard for those of us who have served the company
proudly has already resulted in the resignations of Mr. Hu and Mr. Lee,
two able and expert managers.

We are sorry to have to bring this matter to your attention, but we have
been unable to talk with Mr. Fukuda about it. We also feel that the
situation has become so serious that it is imperative that you, whom we
have always trusted as a sincere and sensitive man, know about it. We
thank you for your time and attention to our plea.

Sincerely yours,

C. Lo

C. Lo, Executive Director,
Finance Division

(and thirteen others)

Exhibit 2. Present and Proposed Organizational Charts for HPS—Taiwan

PRESENT ORGANIZATION

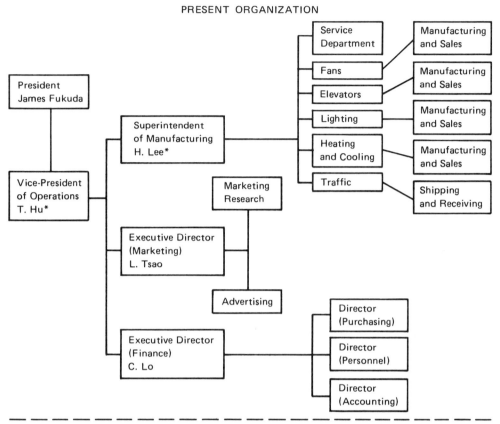

PROPOSED ORGANIZATION

*resigned

Exhibit 3. HPS—Taiwan Balance Sheet (in Thousands of US$)

ASSETS
(as of July 1, 1982)
Current Assets

Cash	1,610
Short-term securities	222
Receivables	1,620
Inventory	11,830
Prepaid expenses	150
Other assets	140
Total Current Assets	15,572

Fixed Assets (at cost)

Buildings	4,182
Machinery and equipment	8,021
Less depreciation	(3,212)
Total Fixed Assets	8,991
Other Assets	410
Total Assets	24,973

LIABILITIES AND SHAREHOLDERS' EQUITY
Current Liabilities

Accounts payable (trade, usance credit and loans)	11,290
Accounts payable (local)	3,150
Loans and current portion of long-term debt	1,130
Other current liabilities	130
Total Current Liabilities	15,700

Long-term debt	3,294
Reserve for depreciation	1,250
Other reserves	120
Duty payable	110
Other liabilities	129
Shareholders' equity	4,370
Total liabilities	24,973

Exhibit 4. HPS—Taiwan Sales by Product Line (All Models), 1976–1981 (in Thousands of US$)

	1976*	1977	1978	1979	1980	1981
Fans	689	724	867	928	831	789
Elevators	1,457	1,763	1,847	2,148	1,658	1,892
Lighting systems	1,408	1,302	1,503	1,429	1,347	1,236
Heating and cooling systems	684	992	1,280	1,564	891	726
Total	4,238	4,781	5,497	6,069	4,727	4,643
Annual growth (in percent)	—	12.8	15.0	10.4	−22.1	−1.8

*includes sales from November and December 1975 (production started Oct. 20, 1975)

Some Points to Keep in Mind

The basic issue in the case is the need for sweeping changes to restore the financial soundness of HPS—Taiwan versus the need to maintain the confidence of the staff. Clearly the financial situation of the Taiwan plant is precarious, but so is the morale of the employees. Fukuda, in assuming responsibility for the subsidiary, is in a difficult position. He sees a number of problems that, in his opinion, need to be solved before any recovery can be achieved. At the same time, he must take into account that he is replacing a seemingly popular Chinese national.

Obviously Fukuda must make some decisions that are not likely to be readily approved of by his all-Taiwanese staff, but he must also consider the timing of those decisions. If he develops an antagonistic relationship between him and his managers, his measures ultimately will have less likelihood of succeeding. Fukuda is evidently aware of this problem and even believes that part of the resentment toward him is because he is a Japanese-American. Nonetheless, he seems to feel that eventually his employees will recognize the need for his changes and figures that renewed financial solvency will outweigh the present difficulties resulting from the transition.

CHECKLIST AND WORKSHEET

In coming to a decision about this case, did you consider the following?

The financial disaster inherited by Fukuda

The stagnant sales trend in heating and cooling equipment

The merits/demerits of both organizational plans

The position of Fukuda as an "outsider"

The importance of the managers' letter to Wolff

Wolff's attitude

What other factors should be considered?

_____

_____

_____

_____

Decision:

_____

_____

_____

_____

DISCUSSION QUESTIONS

I. Background and Dialogue
   1. Summarize the situation at HPS—Taiwan both before and at the time Fukuda took over.
   2. What are Fukuda's qualifications?
   3. What were Fukuda's actions upon being named president? Do they seem logical, given the situation? Why do you think he felt such drastic measures were necessary?
   4. Characterize Fukuda's position in his conversation with Wolff. Is he confident? Upset? Determined? Why does he feel that being a Japanese-American contributes to his problem?

II. Exhibits and Supporting Materials
   1. What are the main objections to Fukuda as outlined in the letter to Wolff (Exhibit 1)? Do the objections seem valid? Objective or subjective? What do you think Lo and the other executives hope to accomplish by writing the letter?
   2. Analyze the organizational charts in Exhibit 2. What seems to be the main purpose of the reorganization? Does it seem to make sense? Why or why not?
   3. Study Exhibits 3 and 4. Given the figures, do you feel that Fukuda was wise in his decision to shut down heating and cooling system manufacturing?
   4. What does Exhibit 4 show about the overall manufacturing sales? Does the decline in HPS sales seem to be confined to a couple of main products? How does this exhibit relate to Fukuda's decision to reorganize?

EXERCISES

I. Select from among the three correct meanings of the italicized word the definition that best defines the word as it is used in the sentence. All of the sentences are drawn from the case.
   1. The Taiwan facility had been losing money at a *precipitous* rate since 1980.
      a. extremely steep
      b. abrupt, sheer, perpendicular
      c. characterized by cliffs
   2. At midyear 1982 the Taipei office reported further *substantial* losses.
      a. basic or essential
      b. of solid character or quality
      c. large quantity
   3. Fukuda had initiated policies that had resulted in *phenomenal* growth.
      a. perceivable by the senses
      b. extraordinary
      c. pertaining to the study of objects or events as they appear in experience
   4. This action, resulting in the layoff of eighteen workers and the reassignment of twelve more, also drew considerable *heat*.
      a. condition of being hot
      b. anger
      c. warmth provided through a heating system

5. Both the vice-president for operations and the plant superintendent *resigned*.
   a. submitted, yielded
   b. gave up a position
   c. withdrew
6. We can't wait for people to be happy with every decision to
   initiate some new measures here.
   a. legislative bills or laws
   b. lengths
   c. actions or procedures
7. It worked fine in Oakland because the operation itself was
   sound.
   a. financially strong
   b. competent, sensible
   c. having no defect as to truth, justice, wisdom, or reason
8. While we understand the need for *sweeping* changes, we take
   issue with two of Mr. Fukuda's actions.
   a. of wide range or scope
   b. overwhelming
   c. moving steadily and forcibly on a target
9. It is clear that their profit *margin* is small.
   a. border or edge
   b. difference between cost and selling price
   c. space around the printed or written page
10. The situation could *backfire* if the product sold is not appropri-
    ate to the client's needs.
    a. have a loud, premature explosion
    b. result in unfavorable consequences
    c. burn an area clear to check a forest fire

II. Write a letter from Wolff to Lo responding to his letter about
    Fukuda. Use information from the Dialogue and the Background to
    help you decide what Wolff's probable position would be.

III. As Fukuda, write a memo to the staff about the management re-
     organization (Exhibit 2). Explain how the new changes will affect
     personnel.

IV. Write a brief summary of the present financial situation at HPS—
    Taiwan. Use information from the Background, Dialogue, and Ex-
    hibit 3 (the balance sheet). From your summary, try to decide
    whether Fukuda's plan seems correct.

V. Prepare a detailed agenda for a meeting Fukuda has arranged with
   the executives of HPS—Taiwan. Take into consideration the fac-

tors brought up in Lo's letter, the present financial crisis, and the proposed changes. Then write a brief introduction that Fukuda might use to get the meeting off to a good start.

VI. Expand the following dialogue between Fukuda and Lo (after Fukuda has talked to Wolff).

Fukuda: Mr. Lo, I must say I'm disappointed that you did not speak to me first before writing to Mr. Wolff.

Lo: _____

_____

Fukuda: I understand that you were upset, but I am only doing what I feel I have to do for the company.

Lo: _____

_____

Fukuda: Why do you call it "Japanese-style management"?

Lo: _____

_____

Fukuda: But Mr. Lo, I'm a second-generation Japanese. I know very little about Japanese management and barely speak Japanese.

Lo: _____

_____

Fukuda: Yes, you're right. Let's talk about the substantive issues here—the reorganization.

Lo: _____

_____

Fukuda: Yes, I understand I may have been a bit hasty in my actions, but given the situation I felt that I had few options.

Lo: _____

_____

VII. Perform the following guided role plays. (See Case 1 Exercises for instructions.)
   1. Fukuda is talking with Wolff after the meeting Fukuda held with the HPS—Taiwan executives to discuss the reorganization.
   2. Lo is offering to resign, telling Fukuda that he can't accept his way of doing business. Fukuda is trying to convince him to stay.
   3. Fukuda is talking to a friend about the situation. The friend offers some frank advice but tries to be sympathetic.

VIII. Debate one of the following issues. (See Case 1 Exercises for instructions.)
   1. Fukuda's measures are unnecessary. He is not taking into account the cultural aspects of the matter, nor is he using sound business tactics.
   2. The best thing for Hanover Public Systems to do would be to close the Taiwan plant.

IX. Write an analysis of the case from the point of view of either Wolff, Fukuda, or Lo.

9 International Carpet Wholesalers

BACKGROUND

Mr. James McHenry, a buyer for International Carpet Wholesalers, a large New York rug importer and distributor, should have been delighted with his day's accomplishments in Rabat, Morocco. He had managed in just twelve hours to come to a tentative agreement with a major Moroccan carpet manufacturer and exporter, Mr. Abdelhadi Hachad, managing director of Société Maroc Tapis (SOMARTA). The agreement, although not yet finalized, provided for the importation of wool from McHenry's firm to SOMARTA in exchange for the export of rugs to International Carpet Wholesalers in New York. The agreement was highly satisfactory to both sides. Mr. Hachad was able to get the raw wool free of import duty since the law allowed for "temporary import" of wool without tariffs providing it was used for manufacturing rugs for export. Mr. Hachad was also pleased because Mr. McHenry had tentatively placed a substantial order for a variety of handmade rugs to be produced over the next year.

Given the obvious success of his day's work, Mr. McHenry should have been pleased. But images of the factory visit kept running through his mind, images of young women, some of whom couldn't have been more than twelve years old, working four or five to a loom. Although the factory was clean, extremely well lighted with daylight, and the girls did not seem unhappy, Mr. McHenry could not help but feel that something was wrong with children of this age working. He has said nothing about this matter to Mr. Hachad but plans to discuss it with him tomorrow.

DIALOGUE: DISCUSSING THE CARPET TRANSACTIONS

Mr. McHenry is meeting with Mr. Hachad in Mr. Hachad's office to finalize the agreement discussed the day before.

Hachad: Mr. McHenry, I had a long discussion with my brother last night, he's a co-owner of the business, you know, and I'm pleased to tell you that we will be able to meet your demand. I should tell you though, that since we'll have to increase our present production capacity a bit, there will be some delay in sending the first shipments.

McHenry: How much of a delay?

Hachad: About ninety days. That's forty-five days longer than you originally specified.

McHenry: Could you send anything in forty-five days?

Hachad: Of course, but not in the quantity you asked for yesterday. Right now, our present capacity is 5,000 square meters a month; 4,000 square meters is already exported to West Germany, and your demand of 2,000 square meters a month in different sizes, shapes, and styles will necessitate not only boosting production but also making some modification in manufacturing.

McHenry: Is that possible? Your factory looks like it's already working to capacity. I can't see how you'd install more looms; they're already so close together.

Hachad: That's no problem. We can simply put more workers to a loom. Also, we do have another small factory in Salé that can take up some of the slack. We also have another workshop where we spin and dye the raw rug wool.

McHenry: Well, I guess how you do it isn't really my business. I take your word that you'll figure it out. By the way, I noticed that a lot of workers in your factory are young girls. Is that customary?

Hachad: Yes. All the factories employ young girls. Does that surprise you?

McHenry: Well, not really. When I bought carpets from Iran, it was much the same, but I don't remember so many *young* girls.

Hachad: Do you know what the working age for apprentices was in Iran?

McHenry: I believe it was fourteen.

Hachad: In Morocco, it's just twelve. Actually, though, those girls don't work for me. We have what's called a *maalema* system here.

McHenry: What's that?

Hachad: Do you remember the older women who were supervising the work teams?

McHenry: Yes.

Hachad: Well, they are called *maalema*. The *maalema* are experienced craftswomen, and they hire their own crews. We only pay the *maalema*. Even the state factories have *maalema*. It's an old tradition here, and one that works quite well. But now, back to business.

McHenry: Sure.

Hachad: About the wool, the question is, when can we begin receiving shipments? As I said yesterday, we could use 80,000 to 100,000 kilos a month.

McHenry: Within forty-five days, providing I can get everything arranged with the Australian supplier within a week or two.

Hachad: That soon?

McHenry: I think so.

Hachad: Well, the sooner we receive it the better. Until it arrives we won't be able to discount the prices as we talked about yesterday. We'll have to keep using the more expensive French wool.

McHenry: Right. I understand that.

Hachad: Regarding the wool and prices, my brother suggested that it might be to both of our advantages to work out a barter agreement. In other words, we will deduct the price of the wool from our finished rugs instead of making a separate transaction for the importing of wool and the exporting of carpets.

McHenry: You mean we charge you nothing for the wool and in turn get a substantial break on the price.

Hachad: Exactly. That way we both save on all the foreign exchange expenses.

McHenry: That's a possibility. The problem is we still have to use foreign exchange to pay for the wool since it comes from Australia. I'd definitely have to run that one by my boss in New York.

Hachad: Well, think about it. How soon can you get an answer on that?

McHenry: Well, I sent her a telex last evening about the terms. She'll get that today. I'll call her this evening to see what I can do about the wool. If I call at 6:00 P.M., it will be 12:00 noon in New York. I might be able to get an answer for you then.

Hachad: Great.

McHenry: If she agrees to the terms, I can get an agreement drawn up once I'm back in New York. Within ten days we should have it all wrapped up.

EXHIBITS AND SUPPORTING MATERIALS

Exhibit I. Telex from McHenry to Ms. Paula Feldman, President of International Carpet Wholesalers

```
RBT8B12      FEB 13, 1984

TO:  P. FELDMAN

FM:  J. McHENRY

RE:  RUG AGREEMENT


MET TODAY WITH A. HACHAD, RABAT MFR. OF HANDMADE CARPETS. HACHAD AGREES

TO SUPPLY 2,000 SQ.M./MONTH. BREAKDOWN AS FOLLOWS:

1,000 SQ.M./MTH MOYEN ATLAS (15/15*) @ 140 DH†/SQ.M.; 300 SQ.M./MTH

RABAT (30/30) @ 300 DH; 400 SQ.M./MTH CHICHAOUA (30/30) @ 300

DH/SQ.M.; 150 SQ.M./MTH PLAIN (PLIED WOOL) 127 DH/SQ.M.; 150

SQ.M./MTH SIMPLE DESIGN (2-COLOR 15/15) @ 135 DH/SQ.M. ROUNDS OR

OVALS AT NO EXTRA COST. ALL PRICES F.O.B.

ALSO WORKED OUT AGRMT FOR IMPORT OF AUSTRALIAN RAW WOOL FROM

HEATHERSTONE. HACHAD WILL TAKE 80,000-100,000 KILOS/MTH. CAN YOU

CONFIRM PER HEATHERSTONE?

RUG QLTY IS HIGH. HACHAD WELL ESTABLISHED. IS CURRENTLY DOING BUS WITH

GERMANS.

PLEASE ADVISE A.S.A.P.
```

*15/15: fifteen horizontal knots and fifteen vertical knots per 10 square centimeters. The more tightly packed (30/30, 40/40), the better the carpet.
†8.0 DH (Dirham) = 1 U.S. dollar.

Exhibit 2. Telex from Feldman to McHenry

```
NY76 BUS FEB 14, 1984

TO: J. McHENRY

FM: P. FELDMAN

RE: RUGS


AGRMT SOUNDS BASICALLY O.K., BUT PLAIN @ 127 DH/SQ.M. AND SIMPLE @ 135

DH/SQ.M. IS HIGH. ALSO NEED QUANTITY BRKDWN ROUNDS/OVALS.


HEATHERSTONE CAN'T CONFIRM 80,000 KILOS/MTH. 50,000 KILOS/MTH MAX

TILL APR, THEN 80,000 K O.K. WHAT IS ADVANTAGE OF EXPORTING WOOL? ARE

PRICES YR. QUOTE FOR MOROCCAN OR HEATHERSTONE WOOL?


CALL ME TOMORROW A.M.


ALL BEST
```

Exhibit 3. Portion of a Letter Sent by McHenry to His Wife

As I montioned, Morocco is fascinating, and I have been quite
successful arranging a deal here. Tho problem, though, is that I feel
terrible about it, and I really don't know what to do. This probably
sounds like a contradiction, but I wish I could somehow undo what I've
done. Why? Because I realize that by getting these rugs at such a good
price I'm directly contributing to the exploitation of children.
Janice, you should see this factory! Little girls, no older than ten or
eleven, some maybe even younger, are working forty-eight hours a week
for 50 cents a day making these rugs. They sit four or five to a loom,
tying knots hour after hour. The owner doesn't even "see" them. The
only people he "employs" are their supervisors, older women called
<u>maalema</u>. The <u>maalema</u> hire their own crews and barely pay these kids.

I've tried to maintain an attitude that this is Morocco and this is the way it's done. At the same time, it really bothers me knowing that I'm perpetuating this situation. From what I hear, most of the factories are the same way, so I just can't go to another. I suppose I should ignore it--I'm supposed to be a businessman after all, not a humanitarian--but I can't. I'm even thinking of telling Paula that I can't get a good deal, but that's nearly impossible since I've already telexed her the details. As you can see, I'm in a quandary. The part of me that is a good businessman says that I should get the best deal I can; the part of me that is a human being says that I should have nothing to do with this exploitation. Of course, if I don't go through with this deal, I better start looking for another job.

I'll let you know what happens. I'll probably leave for Turkey next week . . .

Exhibit 4. Note Sent from McHenry to Hachad

HOTEL RABAT

Dear Mr. Hachad,

I just got a telex from my boss. She says that the wool import deal is going to be hard to arrange. Also, she thinks your prices on plain and simple design (two-color) rugs are too high, so we'll have to do some renegotiation. Please call me when you return from Tangier.

Sincerely,

James McHenry

James McHenry

A Note on the Moroccan Carpet Industry

The Moroccan carpet industry has always occupied a position of importance in the nation's economy. Since the early 1970s, however, exports have risen dramatically to make Morocco the number one exporter of rugs in North Africa. With the increase in production, the character of the industry has changed from an activity centered in small workshops and homes to one of medium-scale industrialization. This industrialization has full government support: Wool may be imported duty free as long as it is used for making carpets for export; export duty and taxes are also waived.

A side effect of this move toward mass production is the employment, on a large scale, of children. Although the legal age of employment is twelve, a study* conducted in 1978 indicated that a great many of the children working (one third of all employees) were under that age. In addition, nearly half of the factories studied had a workweek in excess of the legal forty-eight-hour maximum. The children often worked under *maalema* who were paid on a piecework basis (15–30 DH per sq m). A square meter, depending on the complexity of the design, usually takes one to two days to produce. The children's wages averaged 2–4 DH per day.

The government is aware of the problem and is making efforts to correct it. A first step has been to increase educational opportunities for girls. Factory inspection has also been increased. The problem, though, has been compounded by the fact that more than half of the population of Morocco is under twenty. With such a young population and with an insufficient number of schools, a ready labor supply is at hand at all times.

Some Points to Keep in Mind

This case is multi-faceted. On a straight business level, the situation seems clear: International Carpet Wholesalers needs rugs; Mr. McHenry has been able to arrange a seemingly viable deal with a major producer; the agreement benefits both sides. On a personal and cultural level, though, the situation is not so clear. Is Mr. McHenry overreacting to the methods of another company and the tradition of another country? Beyond that looms another question: What part should a foreign business play in the affairs of another nation?

Some business critics argue that it is the obligation of a company not to do business with a firm that exploits its workers. The recent protest in the United States, for instance, against companies doing business in racially discriminatory South Africa is a good example of this attitude. Others argue that business is business, and that while a company should make efforts to avoid active exploitation of workers, it is neither the right nor the responsibility of a firm to take part in the internal affairs of another country.

*The Anti-Slavery Society, *Child Labor in Morocco's Carpet Industry,* 1978.

For Mr. McHenry, these abstract issues have become personal and concrete. To be a successful businessman, he must accept the conditions of the industry. On a human level, however, this practice is antithetical to his personal views.

CHECKLIST AND WORKSHEET

In coming to a decision about this case, did you consider the following?

McHenry's duty to his employer

McHenry's duty to himself

The ethical question of supporting an exploitative enterprise

The feasibility of the deal itself, especially the supplying of wool to SOMARTA

What other factors should be considered?

_____

_____

_____

_____

Decision:

_____

_____

_____

_____

DISCUSSION QUESTIONS

I. Background and Dialogue
1. Summarize the tentative agreement reached by Hachad and McHenry.

2. What is bothering McHenry? Why do you think that he is so bothered by the situation in Morocco? How is this situation different from the situation in other countries? Or is it?
3. In the Dialogue, how does McHenry bring up the subject of child labor? Does Hachad seem at all concerned about it?
4. What new proposal does Hachad make in the Dialogue?

II. Exhibits and Supporting Materials
1. What is the purpose of McHenry's telex to Feldman (Exhibit 2)?
2. What do we learn about McHenry from Exhibit 3? Why is he in a "quandary"? What does the last sentence in the letter seem to indicate?
3. Why does McHenry need to renegotiate (Exhibit 4)? Do you think it is just the trade arrangements he wants to discuss?
4. What major factors compound the problem of child labor in Morocco (Exhibit 5)? Why is the situation much more complex than it appears to McHenry?

EXERCISES

I. In the exercise below, read over the sentences taken from the case. Using the contextual clues, choose the best definition for the italicized word.
1. He had managed in just twelve hours to come to a *tentative* agreement with a major Moroccan carpet manufacturer.
   a. final
   b. conclusive
   c. provisional
2. Mr. Hachad was able to get the raw wool free of import duty since the law allowed for "temporary import" of the wool without *tariffs*.
   a. import taxes
   b. documents
   c. inspections
3. Your demand of 2,000 square meters a month will necessitate not only *boosting* production, but also making some modifications in manufacturing.
   a. increasing
   b. decreasing
   c. minimizing
4. I'd definitely have to *run that one by* my boss.

a. send it to
b. check it with
c. avoid telling
5. If she agrees to the terms, I can get an agreement *drawn up* once I'm back in New York.
    a. written
    b. sketched
    c. looked at
6. Within ten days we should have it *wrapped up.*
    a. understood
    b. covered up
    c. finalized
7. I'm in a *quandary.* That part of me that is a good businessman says that I should get the best deal I can; the part of me that is a human being says that I should have nothing to do with this exploitation.
    a. bad mood
    b. good situation
    c. dilemma
8. A *side effect* of this move toward mass production is the employment of children.
    a. disadvantage
    b. consequence
    c. advantage
9. Beyond that *looms* another question: What part should a foreign business play in the affairs of another nation?
    a. arises
    b. seems
    c. settles
10. To be a successful businessman, he must accept the conditions of the industry. On a human level, however, this practice is *antithetical* to his personal views.
    a. agrees with
    b. is against
    c. confuses

II. The Background describes both qualitative and quantitative aspects of the case. Quantitative data are regarded as the "hard facts," i.e., information on the material aspects of the case. Qualitative data are the feelings, emotions, and ideas of an individual about those material aspects. List below the main quantitative and qualitative factors regarding the case. Use the information from the Background.

Quantitative Data

Example: James McHenry is a buyer for International Carpet
Wholesalers.

_____

_____

_____

_____

_____

_____

_____

_____

_____

Qualitative Data

_____

_____

_____

_____

_____

_____

_____

_____

_____

_____

III. Expand the dialogue between McHenry and Hachad. This dialogue takes place after Hachad has returned from Tangier and found McHenry's note.

Hachad: I just got your note. What's the problem?

McHenry: _____

_____

Hachad: Let's take one thing at a time. First, about the wool.

McHenry: _____

_____

Hachad: Well, I don't see any problem with waiting until April to receive 80,000 kilos.

McHenry: _____

_____

Hachad: I don't know how we can go much lower than 127 dirhams a square meter. That's really a good price, you know.

McHenry: _____

_____

Hachad: Let me talk to my brother, and I'll see what I can do.

McHenry: _____

_____

IV. Rewrite the two telexes in this case (Exhibits 1 and 2) so that they form complete sentences. You do not need to include the specific rug prices and quantities in Exhibit 1.

V. Exhibit 3 contains a portion of a letter from McHenry to his wife. Start and finish the letter.

VI. Using the information in Exhibit 5, describe the child labor situation in Morocco. Your analysis/summary should contain information based on the facts in the exhibit as well as some recommendations about how the situation could be remedied.

VII. Perform the following guided role plays. (See Case 1 Exercises for instructions.)
1. McHenry is meeting with Hachad to negotiate the final agreement. He brings up the child labor problem again.
2. McHenry is talking to Feldman about the agreement.
3. McHenry is calling his wife to tell her about the trip to Morocco.

VIII. Debate one of the following issues. (See Case 1 Exercises for instructions.)
1. What is the role of Western companies in the Third World? Do these companies perpetuate exploitation?
2. Should a company refuse to do business with a firm that exploits its workers?

IX. Write an analysis of the case from the viewpoint of either Hachad, McHenry, or Feldman.

10 Yoon-Choi Corporation

BACKGROUND

In the spring of 1983 the Yoon-Choi Corporation was pondering the best method of increasing its exports of electronic products, chiefly televisions and radios, to the United States. The Korean corporation, founded in the 1950s, had grown from a small-scale manufacturer of clothing and textiles to a diversified corporation whose activities included machinery, electric, electronic, and textile manufacturing, as well as general trading and real estate development.

In response to the export-priority initiatives instituted by the Park government in the late 1960s, Yoon-Choi expanded its operations from exclusive manufacturing for the domestic market to the point where now over 40 percent of its sales are overseas. In the mid-1970s, Yoon-Choi began exporting televisions and analog clock radios to the United States through its trading division's branch in San Francisco. Most of the sales were to mass retailers, i.e., discount and chain stores, who placed their own brand names on the products. Sales were steady but relatively small, particularly compared to sales by major Japanese and Korean competitors.

In April 1983, Yoon-Choi hired an American marketing consulting firm, Pembroke Marketing Management Associates, to study the situation and present proposals for increasing sales and visibility in the U.S. market.

DIALOGUE: PLANNING A MARKETING STRATEGY

CAST: Woo-Young Jun, International Marketing Director, Yoon-Choi
        Corporation

Phyllis Stevens, Senior Marketing Analyst, Pembroke Marketing
Management Associates

Mr. Jun is discussing electronic products marketing in Ms. Stevens's San
Francisco office.

Stevens: Since receiving the information on your company, I've been
doing some research on likely expansion modes for your firm. I
must say, though, that you've got an impressive company
history.

Jun: Yes, we're proud of ourselves. As you can see, however, we
haven't been as successful with our electronic products in the
U.S. as we would have liked.

Stevens: Well, I have my own views on that matter, but I'd like to hear
what you think your problems have been.

Jun: I'd say we've had three main problems. First, we started late.
By that I mean that our major competitors, Gold-Star, Samsung, and Taihan Electric Wire, got into the electronics market
here long before we did. As a result, they got a jump on us. The
second problem has been that only recently did we start our
own manufacturing of electronic products. Up until 1980 we
relied on subcontractors and therefore couldn't really control
the production as we would have liked. The third problem has
been our distribution methods here in the U.S. We have been
using a dual export mode since we entered the market in 1976.
That is to say, we've exported directly to retailers and indirectly
through Yoon-Choi's trading branch.

Stevens: Your analysis pretty much matches mine. I would say, though,
that your main problem is really with distribution.

Jun: True, but we can't overlook the other problems, particularly the
competitive edge of Gold-Star and Samsung. Gold-Star is especially a problem now that they've opened a factory in Ala-
bama.

Stevens: But that factory is only making color TV sets.

Jun: Right, but their planned production is 120,000 sets a year. That,
combined with their already well-established position, makes
the outlook for color TV sales rather gloomy.

Stevens: I agree, but another way of looking at it is that with Gold-Star
concentrating its efforts on a single product, more territory is
open in other markets.

Jun: But what we aren't sure of right now is which products have
the most sales potential. Plus, we need a comprehensive marketing strategy.

Stevens: Well, from just a limited analysis, it looks like radios and black and white TVs are good bets. You've already established yourself with these lines, and, with some good distribution and representation, I don't see why these products shouldn't take off.

Jun: That brings us back to our other problem: distribution.

Stevens: Exactly. And beyond that, the import mode itself. There are a lot of possibilities, but I would say right now that an attack on all fronts is what you need.

Jun: What do you mean by that?

Stevens: What I'm saying is that you need to increase your marketing channels and your import modes. You've got to go after small and large dealers willing and eager to sell Yoon-Choi's products under your own brand name. At the same time, you've got to beef up sales to mass retailers.

Jun: Hold it. Hold it. Your suggestions are good ones, but what are we talking about in terms of capital, projected sales, and profit margins?

Stevens: I haven't worked it all out yet, but the key here is a volume-oriented pricing policy, not a profit-oriented one. At least, not at the beginning. The more products you've got in front of the consumer, the better your chances are of increasing both visibility and sales. The initial investment, if you choose to adopt a multi-channel marketing policy, is going to be substantial, at least $500,000, but not tremendous. There are, naturally, some ways to cut costs, particularly in promotion, but you've got to be committed to a sizeable initial outlay.

Jun: Well, all this sounds very interesting and possible. Naturally, we want details, but so far, so good.

EXHIBITS AND SUPPORTING MATERIALS

Exhibit 1. Yoon-Choi's 1982 Production and Marketing Costs (Including Sales Figures) for Its Electronic Products Sold in the United States

Average Per Unit Cost for All Models (in Actual US$)	*Product*		
	Black and White TVs	*Radios*	*Car Stereos*
Production costs (including labor and materials)	29.10	11.00	22.96
Overseas transportation and duties	12.20	4.60	10.61
Warehousing and distribution	4.23	2.17	3.45
Local salaries (warehouse help and representatives)	9.06	5.23	8.17
Average markup to dealers (11.0%)	6.00	2.53	4.97
Price after average markup	60.59	25.53	50.16

Actual Sales	*Product*		
	Black and White TVs	*Radios*	*Car Stereos*
Total sales (in millions of US$)	2.67	1.81	1.22
Gross profit (in actual US$)	301,040	196,328	127,932
Total profit (all products) (in actual US$)		625,300	

Exhibit 2. Current and Proposed Distribution Systems for Yoon-Choi Products in the United States

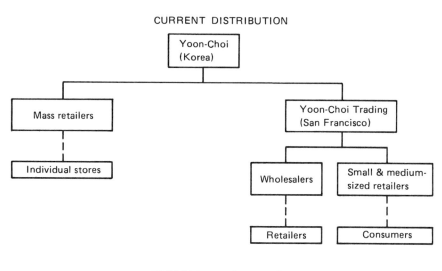

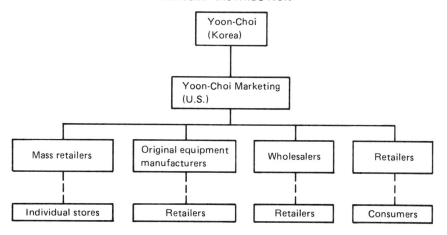

Exhibit 3. The Korean Share in the Total U.S. Consumer Electronics Import, 1971–1980 (in Millions of US$)

Imports to the United States

Exports from Korea

Year	Total Electronics Import A	Consumer Electronics Share (%) B	Consumer Electronics Import C=A×B	Total Consumer Electronics Export D	Share of Export to U.S. (%) E	Consumer Electronics Export to U.S. F=D×E	Korean Share (%) G=F÷C
1971	2,587	50.3	1,301	11	57.5	6	0.5
1972	3,229	55.4	1,789	28	57.2	16	0.9
1973	4,059	49.8	2,021	105	55.9	59	2.9
1974	4,638	43.6	2,022	167	55.4	93	4.6
1975	5,088	43.0	2,188	198	44.3	88	4.0
1976	7,542	44.0	3,318	390	44.9	175	5.3
1977	8,794	42.0	3,693	437	48.3	211	5.7
1978	10,666	43.8	4,672	654	51.7	338	7.2
1979	11,870	35.9	4,261	915	43.1	394	9.2
1980	13,314	33.8	4,500	985	43.0	424	9.4

Source: U.S. Department of Commerce.   *Source:* U.S. Department of Commerce.

Exhibit 4. Import Dependency of the U.S. Consumer Electronics Market by Major Product, 1971–1980 (in Thousands of Units)

	Black and White TVs			Color TVs			Home and Auto Radios		
	U.S. Market	Imports	Dependency	U.S. Market	Imports	Dependency	U.S. Market	Imports	Dependency
1971	7,647	4,166	54.4%	7,247	1,281	17.6%	47,610	34,138	71.7%
1972	8,239	5,056	61.3%	8,845	1,318	14.9%	55,311	43,083	77.9%
1973	7,297	4,989	68.3%	10,071	1,399	13.9%	50,198	45,366	90.4%
1974	6,868	4,659	67.8%	8,411	1,282	15.2%	43,992	39,281	89.3%
1975	4,418	2,975	67.3%	6,219	1,215	19.5%	34,515	31,941	92.5%
1976	5,937	4,327	72.4%	8,194	2,834	34.6%	44,101	41,364	93.8%
1977	6,090	4,908	80.5%	9,341	2,539	27.2%	52,926	43,205	81.6%
1978	6,733	5,931	88.0%	10,674	2,775	26.0%	48,035	43,374	90.3%
1979	6,575	5,874	89.3%	10,042	1,369	13.6%	40,029	33,429	83.5%
1980	6,729	6,172	91.7%	10,779	1,293	12.0%	37,726	33,268	88.2%

Source: U.S. Department of Commerce.

Exhibit 5. Summary of Stevens's Report Regarding Initial Expansion Strategies

A. Distribution

It is essential that a specialist marketing subsidiary be established in the U.S. with the sole purpose of distributing Yoon-Choi's electronic products. This will allow for a concentrated wholesale/retail push as a result of the full-time commitment on the part of the staff. All sales representatives should be placed on salary plus commission.

B. Products

  1. Sales: Continuation of dual brand policy, i.e., Yoon-Choi brand (see Sec. D,6) for small- and medium-size wholesale buyers, private (store) brands for mass retailers or O.E.M.s (original equipment manufacturers). This will allow for high-volume sales to mass retailers and O.E.M.s while simul-taneously building up brand-name image.

  2. Product Selection: Low-end products with a mass consumer orientation. Specifically we recommend aggressive marketing of portable 12″, 13″, and 17″ black and white televisions, portable radios, digital clock radios, car radios, and car cassette stereos. A concentration on marketing low-end products, instead of high-end specialty products, will result in greater sales volume and more rapid brand-name recognition.

C. Pricing Policy

A volume-oriented strategy allows for a competitive low-price policy. This strategy, however, may require Yoon-Choi to increase its present production capacity. With the current surplus inventories of all products targeted for intensive marketing, though, this should not be necessary for at least twelve to eighteen months. Despite our strong recommendation of a volume-oriented pricing plan, we do not suggest that Yoon-Choi sell at a loss in order to build up sales. This policy often backfires if dealers and consumers associate extremely low-priced products with low quality. Furthermore, when prices are raised (as they eventually must be), dealers and O.E.M.s often react negatively and search for new suppliers.

D. Promotion

1. Intensive utilization of trade fairs: With little expenditure consumer electronics shows provide excellent opportunities for increasing Yoon-Choi's visibility and attracting dealer interest and orders. It also allows Yoon-Choi representatives to preview their competitors' new products and to ascertain changing market trends.

2. Special allowances for dealers: High dealer margins, advertising allowances, and point of purchase display subsidies.

3. Trade journal advertising.

4. Gradual introduction of ads in consumer media.

5. Direct mail advertising to dealers and mass retailers.

6. Change of brand name of products from Yoon-Choi to an American name.

Some Points to Keep in Mind

A company must consider a number of factors affecting marketing when initially deciding to sell its products abroad. Most experts generally acknowledge these to be market potential, distribution channels, competition, and consumer behavior and attitudes. These same categories are also important for a company intending to expand its marketing abroad. To ignore these initial factors could prove disastrous.

In this case Yoon-Choi must determine not only what products seem potentially suited to the American market, but also how to increase the sales of these products. The answers to these questions must in turn be weighed against Yoon-Choi's production capacity and investment capabilities.

The consumer electronics market in the U.S. is one of the biggest worldwide, yet is also one of the most competitive. So far, Yoon-Choi has had a limited, but unqualified success in this market. This has led the company to believe that an even greater success is possible. The major questions that must be answered now, though, are whether there is truly potential for increased sales and whether the measures outlined by Stevens will actually accomplish this.

CHECKLIST AND WORKSHEET

In coming to a decision about this case, did you consider the following?

Strength of the competition

The import dependence of the U.S.

Product distribution

Product selection

Investment capital required

Proposed promotion and pricing policies

Yoon-Choi's current performance

What other factors should be considered?

_____

_____

_____

_____

Decision:

_____

_____

_____

_____

DISCUSSION QUESTIONS

I. Background and Dialogue
   1. Describe the basic history of the Yoon-Choi Corporation.
   2. What has been the problem with Yoon-Choi's entry into the U.S. market? Use information from both the Background and Dialogue to support your answer.
   3. What does Stevens think the basic problem with Yoon-Choi really is? How does it differ, if at all, from Jun's?
   4. In the Dialogue, Stevens recommends that Yoon-Choi "attack on all fronts." What does she mean by that?

II. Exhibits and Supporting Materials
   1. Analyze the figures in Exhibit 1. What are the major sources of expense after manufacturing? How would a new distribution system (Exhibit 2) affect these costs?
   2. Study Exhibits 3 and 4. What do they suggest about the U.S. market?
   3. What are the main points of Stevens's report (Exhibit 5)? Do the ideas seem sound? Do they correspond or contradict the information in the preceding tables (Exhibits 4 and 5)?

EXERCISES

I. Fill in the blanks in the following paragraph with the correct word chosen from those below:

adopt   attack   capital   fronts   gloomy   good bets
mode   pondering   visibility   volume-oriented

   After _____ the best method of increasing sales in the

U.S., the Yoon-Choi Corporation decided to hire an American mar-

keting consultant. The consultant studied the situation and pre-

sented a proposal for increasing sales and _____ in the

U.S. market. Yoon-Choi had used a dual export _____

since its entry into the U.S. The consultant advised changing this strategy, particularly in regard to color TVs since the outlook for

color TV sales was _____. Radios and black and white

TVs, however, were considered _____. The consultant

further   advised   Yoon-Choi   to   _____   on   all

_____.   This   meant   that   the   company   needed   to

_____   a   _____   pricing   policy.   The

_____ required   for   the   initial   investment,   though,

was substantial.

II. Summarize the Background

The Yoon-Choi Corporation, in response to the export-priority

_____

_____

Through its trading division _____

_____

_____

Discount and chain stores _____

_____

_____   _____

Compared to their major _____

_____

_____

As a result, _____

_____

III. The Dialogue consists essentially of a discussion of Yoon-Choi's problems and possible solutions. Make a list of these problems with their proposed solutions. Then write a one-sentence statement of each of the problems and the proposed solutions.

> *Example:*   Although Yoon-Choi entered the market late, it can still take advantage of the huge demand for low-cost electronic products.

IV. Write a brief analysis/summary of the information in Exhibit 1. Include information about the most profitable and least profitable products, the relation between production/transit costs and selling prices, and the relation between total sales and gross profit. From your analysis, which is the most profitable and easily marketed product?

V. Interpret the information in Exhibit 4 regarding the U.S. dependency on foreign imports. Given your analysis, which is (are) the best market(s) for foreign imports?

VI. Expand the dialogue between Stevens and Jun (after Jun has received Stevens's report).

> *Jun:*   I'm not clear on why you feel we should establish a marketing subsidiary in the U.S. Why can't our present trading division handle it?

> *Stevens:* _____
>
> _____

> *Jun:*   But that seems unnecessary.

> *Stevens:* _____
>
> _____

> *Jun:*   Okay. Let's leave that issue alone for now. What about the product selection?

> *Stevens:* _____
>
> _____

> *Jun:*   Well, I agree with a volume-oriented pricing policy, but

our competitors also have adopted the same strategy. How can we compete, effectively and aggressively?

Stevens: _____

_____

Jun: But isn't that much advertising going to be terribly expensive?

Stevens: _____

_____

VII. Perform the following guided role plays. (See Case 1 Exercises for instructions.)
1. Stevens is presenting the new distribution plan (Exhibit 2) to Jun.
2. Jun is talking with Stevens about preparing an ad campaign for Yoon-Choi's product and discussing possible name changes.
3. Jun is talking with the San Francisco office about adopting a new strategy to market the products more aggressively.

VIII. Debate one of the following issues. (See Case 1 Exercises for instructions.)
1. The U.S. market is so saturated with low-end, volume-priced imports that it makes little sense for Yoon-Choi to invest heavily in trying to corner a share of this market.
2. The practice of "dumping" (flooding a market with underpriced goods) is counterproductive for both buyer and seller. Furthermore, laws should be passed to prevent this practice.

IX. Write an analysis of the case from the point of view of either Jun or Stevens.

Glossary of Business and Technical Terms

The definitions of these terms are given within the context in which they are used in the case. Alternative meanings also exist for a number of words.

Acceptance   A written order from a buyer's bank to a seller's bank for payment to the seller. Also called bill of exchange.

Accounts payable   The amount of money owed by a business for goods and services bought in everyday transactions. Accounts payable generally do not include long-term debts.

Accounts receivable   The amount of money owed to a business by its customers.

Analog input   Information sent to a computer in analog form (electromechanical rather than digital) from devices that measure physical quantities or processes.

Annual growth   The amount of growth, measured in financial terms, of a company over the course of one year.

Application-specific software   Computer programs designed to perform one specific task.

Assets   Any property or item (including land, cash, machinery, investments) owned by a company that has money value.

Audit   An inspection of accounting records and procedures conducted by a trained person, an auditor, to check on their accuracy.

Barter   The exchange of goods or services for goods or services without the use of money.

Bid   In construction, an offer, usually in response to a request from a purchaser, to do a project for a specific price.

Brand name   A name or symbol that identifies a product as having been made by a particular company, for example, IBM and Coca Cola.

Breach of contract   The violation of a legal contract by one or both of the signers.

Broker   An agent authorized by a company to represent it in certain business transactions.

Campaign   A business strategy used to market and sell a company's product or products. An advertising campaign usually consists of a series of ads that attempt to acquaint potential buyers with the product.

Capital   The total assets of a firm. Operating capital is the amount of money available for running the day-to-day operations of a firm. Investment capital is the amount of money available for investment.

Chain store   One of a group of stores owned by one company which carry similar merchandise.

C.I.F.   Cost including freight. A term used in international trade to indicate that the price for goods includes insured transportation to the destination designated by the buyer. *See* F.O.B.

Commodity   Any physical good such as food, machinery, minerals, or finished products.

Cost overruns   The amount of money spent in excess of the amount of money originally projected.

Countertrade   The exchange of goods for goods.

Curing room   In tire building, a room in which a tire is molded, shaped, and vulcanized under heat and pressure. These are the last steps in tire production.

Current assets   Any asset that can be easily turned into money, such as cash on hand, notes, accounts receivable, and inventories.

Current liabilities   The amount of money currently owed by a company to other businesses or individuals. Current liabilities include salaries, short-term loans, accounts payable, and taxes.

Direct mail advertising   The practice of sending promotional material through the mail to a selected group of potential buyers. Direct mail lists consist of the names and addresses of prospective customers.

Distributor   An individual or firm selling a manufacturer's product.

Dual export The practice of exporting goods to both wholesalers and retailers.

Earnings per share The amount of money earned by a shareholder during a fixed period on one share of stock.

Equity The excess of a company's assets over its liabilities.

Eurodollar A U.S. dollar held outside the United States, usually as a deposit in a commercial bank.

Exclusive distribution agreement An agreement that gives one company the only right to distribute a manufacturer's products in a specified geographical area.

Feasibility study A report that evaluates a proposed or contemplated action to determine whether it is physically and economically desirable.

Fiscal Of or related to money.

Fixed assets Assets that cannot easily be turned into money, such as land, equipment, buildings, and long-term investments.

F.O.B. Free on board. A term used in international trade to indicate that the price for goods does not include transportation to the buyer's destination. *See* C.I.F.

Gross sales The total sales of a company within a given period before taxes and other expenses.

H-steel In construction, a long steel beam that when looked at from either end appears to be H-shaped.

Hardware/software In computer terminology, hardware is the physical computer itself; software, any program run on the computer.

Industrial microcomputer A special type of microcomputer with large storage and very sophisticated data-processing capabilities for use in industrial operations. It is usually used for control or monitoring of manufacturing or mechanical processes.

Inventories The total amount of materials owned by a company, either as finished products or raw materials.

Joint venture A business partnership formed for the purpose of carrying out a specific project or projects.

Layoffs The temporary or permanent removal of employees from a company, usually because of production changes.

Liabilities The amount of money owed by a company to other businesses or individuals.

Liquidation   The dissolving of a company through the sale of its assets. Partial liquidation involves selling a portion of a company's assets, usually to meet obligations.

Maestro   Spanish for "master," a title usually given to a master craftsman.

Manufacturer's warranty   A written guarantee issued by the manufacturer certifying that the product purchased is free from defects. If the product is found to be defective, it is the responsibility of the manufacturer (or manufacturer's representative) to repair or replace the product.

Margin (profit margin)   The difference between the buying and selling price.

Mechanical   In the graphic arts, a board prepared for offset reproduction with all art work and type pasted down ready for reproduction.

Middleman   Any intermediary between the manufacturer and ultimate consumer of goods, such as a wholesaler who buys goods from a manufacturer and sells them to retailers.

Multiprocessing   A special feature that allows a computer to process data from several different sources at the same time.

Multitasking   An advanced feature that allows a computer to perform several tasks simultaneously.

Net actual change   The actual change after expenses, measured in currency, of a company's position or investments between one fixed period and another.

Notes payable   The amount owed by a company to a bank on its short-term loans.

Parallel import   A situation in which identical products are imported by different importers, but with only one company having the right to do so.

Piecework   A manufacturing arrangement in which workers are not paid an hourly wage but are paid a specific amount for each "piece," or product, they produce.

Prepaid expenses   Expenses incurred for future benefit, such as rent, taxes, or insurance paid in advance.

Price war   A situation in which two or more competitors in the same market systematically reduce the price charged for similar goods in order to maintain or gain a larger share of the market.

Profit-oriented pricing   The pricing of goods at the maximum possible level in order to gain the maximum amount of profit.

Pylons   Steel bars used for constructing a framework.

Real-time   The ability of a computer to gather, process, and make available information fast enough to control an outgoing process.

Retail sales   Sales to the final consumer. A retail store is a store selling to individual consumers.

Retaining wall   A wall constructed for the purpose of providing support or for holding in place earth, water, mud, etc.

Revenue   The income received by a business from the sale of its goods or services.

Sales forecast   A projection of what a company's sales are likely to be in the future. A sales forecast is usually based on a combination of factors affecting the market.

Share   A portion of interest in a company. The smallest investment is one share of stock.

Shareholder   An individual or corporation owning a portion of a company through an investment in the form of shares.

Shareholder's equity   The amount of a company's assets owned by the shareholders.

Short-term securities   Investments in bonds and/or money held in various types of interest-paying bank accounts which can be quickly converted to cash.

Siesta   A Spanish term describing a two- or three-hour period in the middle of the day during which most shops and businesses are closed.

Specification   In construction, the pre-specified conditions by which finished work is acceptable.

Subcontractor   An individual or firm hired by the contractor to perform specialized work such as masonry, plumbing, wiring, or flooring.

Subsidiary   A business firm that is controlled by another company (the parent company) that owns most or all of its stock.

Tariff   A tax imposed by a government on imported goods.

Telex   A telegraphic method, often used internationally, of sending a printed message from one place to another by teleprinter. Telex is also used to describe the physical message itself.

Title   A certificate of ownership.

Transit items   Deposits by customers of cash items such as checks, money orders, and acceptances drawn on banks outside of the city in which they have an account. Such deposits must be transmitted from the collector's bank to the payer's bank for payment.

Volume-oriented pricing   A policy in which goods are priced at a minimal profit level in order to sell large quantities.

Wholesalers   Middlemen who buy goods from a manufacturer for resale to retailers.